I loved the way Dave and Claudia tol[...] That's what made this marriage book [...] each year.

— Mike Yorkey, Editor, *Focus on the Family* magazine

Through the personal sharing of their own marital experience, Dave and Claudia make available a wealth of ideas, practical suggestions and inspiration for couples who care about their marriage and want to make it strong, deeper, and more fulfilling.

— Dr. Vera Mace, Author and co-founder of the
American Association of Marriage and Family Therapy (A.A.M.F.T.)
and the Association for Couples in Marriage Enrichment (A.C.M.E.)

Dave and Claudia Arp are good people with a powerful message to help make our marriages and families better. Warm, humorous, and insightful, the Arps share information that is practical and enriching.

— Dr. Nick Stinnett, Professor of Family Studies,
University of Alabama, Co-author of *Secrets of Strong Families*

The Arps are an outstanding resource in the area of marriage enrichment and an asset for the military. *Ten Great Dates* will breathe new life and joy into relationships. A practical and timely answer to a world seeking the path of growth and enrichment.

— Larry L. Eakes, Chaplain (MAJ), United States Army

With wisdom, wit, and sympathetic understanding, the Arps help us to revitalize our marriages with practical insights. Wonderfully readable, as well as profoundly on target psychologically.

— Michael O'Donnell, Ph.D.,
International Family Life Institute, Inc.

Also by David and Claudia Arp

The Second Half of Marriage

The Love Book

Where the Wild Strawberries Grow

The Ultimate Marriage Builder

52 Dates for You and Your Mate

60 One-Minute Marriage Builders

60 One-Minute Family Builders

60 One-Minute Memory Makers

52 Ways to Be a Great Mother-in-Law (Claudia Arp)

Almost 13 (Claudia Arp)

Beating the Winter Blues (Claudia Arp)

Sanity in the Summertime (coauthored with Linda Dillow)

The Big Book of Family Fun (coauthored with Linda Dillow)

For more information about Marriage Alive resources or to schedule the Arps for a Marriage Alive Seminar or other speaking engagement contact:

Marriage Alive International
51 West Ranch Trail
Denver, CO 80465
Phone: (888) 690-6667
Email: mace@marriagealive.org
Website: www.marriagealive.com

To receive a fun, weekly marriage builder from the Arps, subscribe (free) to Zondervan's e-mail service by sending a "subscribe zphlove" message (without quotes) to lists@info.harpercollins.com with nothing in the subject line (AOL subscribers type a hyphen there). Questions? zpub@zph.com.

10 GREAT DATES

to Energize
Your Marriage

The Best Tips from the Marriage Alive Seminars

DAVID & CLAUDIA ARP

ZONDERVAN™

GRAND RAPIDS, MICHIGAN 49530

ZONDERVAN™

10 Great Dates to Energize Your Marriage
Copyright © 1997 by David and Claudia Arp

Requests for information should be addressed to:

Zondervan, *Grand Rapids, Michigan 49530*

Library of Congress Cataloging-in-Publication Data

Arp, Dave.
    10 great dates to energize your marriage : the best tips from the Marriage Alive
seminars / David and Claudia Arp.
       p.   cm.
    Includes bibliographical references.
    ISBN: 0–310–21091–7 (pbk.)
    1. Marriage.   2. Communication in marriage.   3. Dating (Social customs)
4. Marriage—Religious aspects—Christianity.   I. Arp, Claudia.   II. Title.
HQ734.0.A685 1997
646.7'8–dc21   96–50967
                                                    CIP

Published in association with the literary agency of Alive Communications, Inc., 7680 Goddard
Street, Suite 200, Colorado Springs, CO 80920.

This book is a resource for marriage enrichment, not a substitute for needed professional
counseling. If some of the exercises contained in this book raise issues for you or your spouse
that cannot be easily resolved, we urge you to seek professional help.

Interior design by Sherri L. Hoffman

Printed in the United States of America

---

  02 03 04 05 06 /❖ DC/ 20 19 18 17 16 15

*To our dear friend and mentor,
Vera Mace, and in memory
of her husband, David Mace*

Contents

Acknowledgments

We gratefully acknowledge the contributions of the following people:

- All the couples who have participated in our Marriage Alive seminars over the years and who have shared with us your struggles and success stories;
- Our dear friend and mentor, Vera Mace, for David's and your life work in helping marriages succeed and for your input, wisdom, and insight in helping us with the content of this book;
- The many other researchers and authors we quoted, for your sound work, which gives a solid base for the cause of marriage enrichment;
- Our friend and publisher, Scott Bolinder, for your belief in us and your vision to help couples revitalize their marriage, which turned our dream into a reality;
- Our editor, Sandy Vander Zicht, for sharing your expertise and patiently nudging us on;
- Development editor, Mary McNeil, for your excellent editing and for making this book so much fun;
- Jody Langley, for making this book look like the fun it is;
- Our own Arp "in-house" team—Laurie Clark, for helping to make the message of marriage enrichment clear and easy to grasp; Jonathan and Autumn Whiteman Arp, for participating in your own "ten great dates" and helping with the video component of this resource;
- The Zondervan New Media department, especially Mark Hunt and Jeff Bowden, for your creative help in putting together the complementing video resource;
- Tom Rowland, Jerry Conrad, Dick Dodson, John Heiser, and all the great people at Rowland Productions for making *10 Great Dates* come alive on video;

- Doug Cline at Centel Productions for your creative music component;
- The Maclellen Foundation for your generous grant that helped underwrite the video production, so that groups of any size can enrich their marriages;
- Our literary agent, Greg Johnson of Alive Communications, for being our advocate and encouraging us along the way.

A Personal Note
from Claudia and Dave

❧ ❧

*F*lying over the glaciers and ice fields of the Alaskan Kenai Peninsula in a small six-seater twin-engine Cessna pushed our limits of exciting dates. Certainly this was one date neither of us ever considered! Some call it "flight-seeing"; Claudia renamed it "fright-seeing."

While dating is a habit we've had for years, we never know where we will end up on a date. Our "flight-seeing" date started when our friend Eileen asked us, "How would you like to experience a great date in Alaska?" Being an adventurous couple, we responded, "Wow! How do we sign up?"

The next thing we knew, we were on a plane headed to Anchorage, Alaska. Of course there was a catch—while in Alaska, we agreed to lead several marriage and family seminars. That's where we met another dating couple, Clint and Sally, who told us their story:

"After a lackluster first ten years of marriage we both agreed we needed to jazz up our marriage, but we weren't sure how to go about it," Clint told us.

"I looked for resources and discovered a book of ten dates," Sally said. "Clint wasn't so sure dating would help us—he was the original 'dragee,' but after some friendly persuasion, he agreed to try."

Clint continued the story. "I was hesitant. Previously, we tried working through other 'marriage manuals' with little success. I'm a teacher, and the last thing I wanted was more assignments and work. But I have to admit, these dates were different—they were fun, and we picked up marital skills that pushed our relationship a couple of notches higher."

"Having regular dates," Sally said with a big smile, "has kept our relationship vital and alive for more than a decade! We gladly recommend dating to every couple! As a matter of fact, we gave at least ten copies of that original dating book to friends."

COME FLY WITH ME!

*A*re you looking for a little pizzazz? Do you want your marriage to fly high? You don't have to go all the way to Alaska to add excitement, but you do need to find some time. When was the last time you talked to your spouse for thirty uninterrupted minutes? Would you like to have more fun with your spouse? Is dating something you only did before you were married?

We believe that having a healthy, growing marriage relationship requires friendship, fun, and romance. And there's no better way to encourage all of these things than having dates! Great dates are more than going to see a movie and tuning out the world for a while. Great dates involve communicating with one another, reviving the spark that initially ignited your fire, and developing mutual interests and goals that are not focused on your careers or your children. Great dates can revitalize your relationship. We've got the proof!

TEN DATES FOR MATES

*F*or over three decades we have worked hard on our own marriage. Through our own successes and failures and through research and study, we discovered principles that helped us build a strong marriage partnership. Amazingly, we found that one key indicator of an enriched marriage is having a strong "couple" friendship. And what better way to build a great couple friendship than to date your mate?

So, to help couples begin dating and make their relationship a priority, we put together our Marriage Alive seminar and wrote *Ten Dates for Mates* (this was the book Clint and Sally found), and later we wrote *The Marriage Track*. For over twenty years we have shared these principles through our books and seminars, and have helped many couples build strong, solid marriage partnerships through dating their mate, couples like Ruth and David and Alicia and Jeff.

"We had been married for nine years," Ruth told us, "when we found your book and started dating. Through our initial ten dates, we learned how to make life smoother and resolve conflicts more easily. Dating jump-started our marriage. Years later, we're still dating, and our dates continue to give us the opportunity to step out of our hectic life and work on improving our marriage. Plus, dating is fun! We've even done some crazy things on our dates like walking in the rain and getting totally soaked, or dancing in the aisle of a supermarket to the music over the speaker system, performing for all the curious and fascinated senior citizens!"

"Dating revolutionized our marriage," Jeff said. "Years ago when I was in medical school, our marriage was foundering. Twenty-hour workdays didn't help. Alicia and I were becoming strangers and were well aware of the divorce statistics in the medical community. We knew we needed to do something to reignite our relationship. About that time we found your book *Ten Dates for Mates*. The book revitalized our marriage when it was at a low point. Having ten consecutive dates started a habit. Years later we are still dating! We even started our own dating club with our friends and have given away many of your books. Our personal copies have long since been tattered. How can we get more?"

We were happy to tell Jeff that though the original *Ten Dates for Mates* is history—except for battered copies—we were putting together ten new, improved dates to revitalize marriage relationships.

From our work in marriage enrichment and our interaction with couples over the years, we have crafted ten great dates based on ten skills that will infuse your marriage with new vitality. Each date will focus on a skill needed to have an alive, growing marriage.

The first three dates focus on how to develop your own marriage coping system. Being committed to grow and change together over the years mandates having a workable communication system and having the skills to process anger and resolve conflict in a positive way. Other dates will help you encourage each other, develop a solid partnership based on your individual strengths, and build a creative love life. You'll be challenged to work together and share responsibilities, to enrich your marriage while parenting your children, and to develop spiritual intimacy. Then you'll learn how to have an intentional marriage. As you experience your ten great dates, you can revitalize your relationship—and have fun in the process!

AND NOW THE FUN BEGINS!

The second part of this book is your personal dating guide. If you're not sure where to go or what to do, don't worry! We've included many creative suggestions—both from us and from other dating couples.

While the Marriage Alive dating plan is designed for couples, it is also appropriate for groups. If you know you need the pressure of being committed to others, recruit other couples to go through these dates with you. A complete video curriculum is also available for starting your own *Couples' Nights Out.*™

HOW TO MAXIMIZE YOUR DATING EXPERIENCE

*R*ead the corresponding chapter before each date. You will find a brief chapter summary in each date's guide to use if either spouse is unable to read the entire chapter. Also in the dating guide you'll find discussion starters and short exercises that will help you focus on improving your relationship.

Then date your mate. In a relaxed dating atmosphere (preferably away from interruptions) you will have the opportunity to talk, to connect, to fine-tune a specific skill to enhance your marriage. It's the practical application during each date that will make the difference. Your ten great dates will be fun and will make your marriage come alive with new vitality, energy, and excitement.

WILL IT REALLY MAKE A DIFFERENCE?

*T*he difference between reading a book and having your marriage enriched is your involvement! Statistics suggest that it takes three weeks to break or start a habit and six weeks to feel good about it. We suggest ten dates to grow in intimacy to improve your relationship. Plus, dating will become a new habit that will benefit your marriage long after you've finished this book.

I'M CONVINCED! HOW CAN I START?

*T*he following ten steps will help you begin your dating experience on a positive note:

1. Agree to have ten dates with your mate. It really doesn't matter who found the book and whose idea it was. The important thing is that both of you are willing to have ten dates to enrich your marriage.

2. Schedule your dates and write them in your calendar.

3. Clear your schedule. This may include getting a sitter and putting off some seemingly urgent tasks.

4. Plan for possible interruptions. Despite the best planning, at times children get sick or other unexpected problems arise, and you will have to change your plans. When this happens, reschedule your date for the same week, if possible, and persevere. Hang in there and value your time together. Our friends Florence and Charlie know what it means to persevere. They planned a weekend away to go through this book. Charlie made the hotel reservations and Florence arranged for a sitter and cooked food ahead. But at the last minute, their daughter broke out with chicken pox. The second time, the sitter got sick! Only after the third try did their plans actually work.

5. Anticipate each date. Let your spouse know you're looking forward to time together. Be clever. Send notes, and give hints that you're anticipating a great date with your mate.

6. Before the date, read the short chapter and note key topics to discuss. If you fill out the short exercise before the date, you'll have more time for intimate conversation. But if not, you can do the exercise during the date.

7. Follow our simple guide for each date. One caution: Don't use date time to deal with problems. Also, if you have children, leave them with the sitter, and don't utter their names until your date is over!

8. Stay positive! Hold hands. Cuddle. It's hard to be negative when you're holding hands. Plan each date around something you enjoy doing. For us, if we really want to talk, we have a "Walk and Talk" date and go to a park, or to our favorite coffee shop for two cups of cappuccino.

9. Be future focused. Even though you may discuss past issues, focus on the future. Ask yourself questions such as "What have we learned that can make a difference next week and next month?"

10. Get started! Good marriages take time. We've found that the key to building a successful marriage is actually taking the time to work on the relationship. Perhaps, like us, you keep waiting to win a two-week cruise for two, or for the kids to grow up,

or for twenty-four hours of uninterrupted time to be miraculously dropped into your lap, complete with coupons for a candlelit dinner for two and a night away at a posh hotel. We would all like gifts such as these, but in reality, most of us live in a perpetual time crunch. That's why we designed these dates to be simple, practical, interactive, and fun.

MAKE A COMMITMENT

Ten great dates will only make a difference if you experience them. Like most things worthwhile, growing an enriched marriage requires time. Good intentions aren't enough. A written commitment can help you carry through with good intentions. Use the commitment form that follows to record your promise to each other. You'll be glad you took the time to encourage, build up, and appreciate one another. Remember, yesterday is past and tomorrow is in the future. Today is the only gift of time you've been given. That's why it is called "the present." So give each other the present of *Ten Great Dates*!

MAKING A COMMITMENT

I agree to invest time in building our marriage by experiencing *Ten Great Dates.*™

Signed:

Husband_____

Wife _____

Date _____

Part One

10 Great Dates

Date One

❧❧❧

Choosing a
High-Priority Marriage

*W*hy do we do this to ourselves?" Claudia asked in total frustration. "No one plans a blowout," Dave responded as he pulled the car to the side of the road. His logic was no comfort to Claudia. She was past the point of being objective or logical. As we sat in our disabled car, we were totally frustrated. Our three weeks in Europe weren't working out the way we had hoped.

Leading back-to-back Marriage Alive seminars in two different countries had left us exhausted. And then that day's adventures just added to our stress. After eight hours in the car, we had spent the evening talking with Tim and Francis, parents of four children, about how they could survive their children's adolescence.

Now, late at night, all we wanted to do was get back to our hotel and hit the sack. But as we drove up the dark, winding, Alpine road, we hit something else. The sudden jolt and rough ride confirmed our fears—a sharp rock had caused a blowout.

Timing couldn't have been worse. The night air was frigid; our compact rental car was loaded with our luggage and food. The next morning we were to begin a week's vacation in the Austrian Alps. But there we sat! Our hotel was not within walking distance. It was cold, and we were too tired to unload the car to search for a spare tire, so we drove on to the hotel with the flat tire. The next morning, before we could start our vacation, Dave had to replace the tire.

But our story doesn't end here. Later that day we made it to our mountain chalet. Two hours after we arrived, Claudia noticed that her back was becoming more and more uncomfortable. She tried walking it off, but the pain increased. We spent the whole week doing nothing because Claudia literally couldn't move.

Marriage sometimes reminds us of that Austrian experience. We travel overloaded and stressed-out. We keep talking about finding time up the road to regroup and relax, but before we reach that point, we have a blowout. Maybe you haven't experienced a major blowout in your relationship. It's more like a slow leak. But you know that if you want to keep growing together, you need to take some time to work on your relationship. Throughout our thirty-four-year marriage we have experienced both.

OUR MARRIAGE CRISIS

Years ago we came to a critical point in our marriage. In 1973, we moved to Germany for Dave's job as a consultant for an international organization. Dave was enthusiastic about the move; Claudia was not. She missed home, family, friends, and Pampers. We had three small children and no baby-sitters or "Mom's Day Out" opportunities. We didn't speak German yet and had no telephone for eight months.

The one thing we did have was time together. But while we were physically together, emotionally we were miles apart. We felt disconnected. Alone. Isolated. Before moving to Germany, we had prided ourselves on having a great marriage. But over the years the little barnacles had built up on our marriage ship. They became glaringly evident when the waves of activity subsided. Suddenly we had time to talk—time to face issues previously ignored.

One morning as we stared at each other across the kitchen table, we realized how far apart we had drifted.

"Dave, I don't feel like I even know you anymore," Claudia said, looking across the table at Dave and bursting into tears. "I don't feel comfortable here. I can't speak German. Our boys have no friends, and whatever happened to our friendship? Now that we actually have time to talk to each other, what do we have to say?"

"Claudia, I know the stress and pressures of moving a family of five halfway across the world in six weeks have taken their toll," Dave said. "But I also know we love each other. We can work things out."

The one thing we agreed on that morning was our need to regroup. We loved each other and were committed to our marriage, but the recent months had pushed us apart instead of pulling us together. We both wanted to renew our relationship and move closer to each other.

That Saturday morning, over two cups of coffee, we agreed to start over. We began to talk about our relationship and to focus on positive memories. Our conversation drifted back to the time we met. We talked again about what had attracted us to each other—Dave's easygoing personality and listening ear, Claudia's endless ideas and energy. (Somehow, after marriage, we had redefined those attractions as Dave's being too slow and Claudia's overcommitment and lack of focus.) We talked about our first date and about our certainty three weeks later that "this was it!" We found ourselves reliving a long-forgotten part of our lives. And as we focused on the positive memories, we were able to tackle the problems of the present. For the first time we took a good look at our marriage and talked through our relationship—where it appeared to be heading and where we wanted it to go. We identified three marriage goals.

THREE MARRIAGE GOALS

Our first goal was to look at and evaluate where our marriage was at the present. Without realizing it, we had grown apart—both felt alone and isolated. It is possible to be married and still be all alone—to be physically close but emotionally miles away. In thinking back over our marriage history before we moved to Germany, we realized that the times we felt most alone and disconnected were the times we were too busy. We used to kid about having a front-door relationship. As one of us came in the door, the other handed off the kids and left. Both of us were overcommitted and overinvolved in activities outside the home. We kept saying we needed to find time to talk through some issues, but we had difficulty actually finding that time—until we moved to Germany. Then we didn't know what to do with it. We needed to focus.

Our second goal was to set some long-term marriage goals—to look at where we wanted our marriage to be in six months, in one year, in five years. What did we want our marriage to look like when we had been married for fifty years? We began to set some bite-sized goals and to work toward each one—step by step. As we reached one, it encouraged us to continue.

One of our first steps was coming up with a more equitable plan for our evenings. Dave agreed to begin bathing and reading to our boys while Claudia did the kitchen cleanup. After being with the boys all day, she was ready for a break. Also, we invested in an automatic dishwasher, which, in Germany at that time, was considered a luxury; for us, it was a marriage saver. After the boys were in bed and the kitchen was tidy, we'd have time to be together.

It didn't always work out, but once a week we tried to put the boys to bed early and have a quiet candlelit dinner for two. Sometimes we were just too tired to talk, but other times our late dinners were a real catalyst for intimate conversations and sharing. And as difficult as it was to find sitters, we began to schedule monthly dates.

Our third goal was to learn some new skills or to learn to use the old ones we already knew but didn't use, such as really listening to each other and not just thinking about what we wanted to say when the other stopped talking. We also worked on dealing with anger and conflict. It was hard not to attack each other, but when we took time to calm down and tried resolving issues together, our relationship was strengthened. Often, the problem wasn't just knowing what to do, but doing what we knew! Setting goals really helped us get turned around. We were able to reaffirm that we had a great partnership, but it took lots of work, and it didn't happen overnight. We discovered marriage is a journey—not a destination—and today we still work to make our marriage a high priority.

REMEMBER WHEN?

*Y*ears ago in Germany, we found that focusing on our good memories reminded us of how important our marriage was. And just reliving our romance reignited the spark. Has the romance dissipated in your marriage? Stop for a moment and think about that time when you couldn't bear to be apart. Do you remember the first time you ever saw each other? We won't forget the day we first met. Claudia was thirteen, and fifteen-year-old Dave threw her into the swimming pool with her clothes on! But we were first attracted to each other when we met after

Claudia graduated from high school. After finishing his freshman year at Georgia Tech, Dave was again spending the summer with his grandmother who lived in the same small North Georgia town where Claudia grew up. Dave's impish nature was still in full force, but he was also fun-loving, adventurous, and a college man! Claudia's vivaciousness, enthusiasm for life, and the twinkle in her eyes were irresistible to Dave.

What attracted you to your mate when you first met? What do you think attracted your mate to you? What about your first date? Do you remember the first time you talked about getting married? The first time we seriously talked about getting married was in the middle of our college years. The Cuban missile crisis traumatized our nation—and us! The Russian missiles were headed for Cuba, and the United States had its blockade in position. We were convinced that the world was going to blow up and that we might never get to live together as husband and wife. So two months later, at Christmas, we got married—without the benefit of premarriage seminars, counseling, or any of the other helps available today.

What do you remember about your wedding day? We reacted totally differently. Claudia was so nervous that she hardly slept the whole night before. Dave took a nap an hour before the ceremony and would have missed the wedding if his dad hadn't awakened him!

Think about the first place you called "home." Our first home was a tiny basement apartment. We were still in college and had all hand-me-down furniture, including a bed with too-short slats that kept falling in!

Think about the times you have felt especially close to your mate. It might have been at the birth of a child, during an intimate weekend away, or on a walk on the beach.

It's fun to think back into our history and remember the excitement of that time when we realized we were in love. Memories help us to remember just how important our marriage is and why we want to keep nurturing our relationship. They motivate us today to make our marriage a high priority. We hope revisiting your memories will help affirm that your marriage is also a high priority! So how can we keep our marriages growing?

THREE PRINCIPLES FOR A HIGH-PRIORITY MARRIAGE

*I*n our national survey of long-term marriages, we found three common strands in those marriages that are alive and healthy. First, the marriage relationship comes before other relationships; second, both spouses are committed to growing and changing together; and third, they work at staying close. In this chapter we want to consider how these three principles will help you make your marriage a high priority. Ignoring any one of them will be unhealthy for your marriage.

Put Your Marriage First

When we marry, we promise to stand by each other in sickness and in health till death do us part. It is both a physical act and an attitude of preferring each other above all others.

At a recent wedding, the unique presentation of the couple by both sets of parents impressed us with how important it is to affirm our marriage as our priroity relationship from the very beginning. It went something like this:

> *Celebrant: The union of this couple brings together two family traditions, two systems of roots, in the hope that a new family tree may become strong and fruitful. Theirs is a personal choice and a decision for which they are primarily responsible. Yet their life will be enriched by the support of the families from which each comes. Will you parents encourage this couple in their marriage?*
>
> *Parents: We will.*
>
> *Celebrant: Do you celebrate with them the decision they have made to choose each other?*
>
> *Parents: We do.*
>
> *Celebrant: Will you continue to stand beside them, yet not between?*
>
> *Parents: We will.*

Patricia told us, "Harry and I didn't get along well at all in the first months of our marriage. After one ghastly fight, I remember calling my mother, wanting to go home. My mom refused. 'You married Harry,' she told me. 'You've just got to work it out.'"

Running home to Mama was not an option—Patricia had to learn how to work things out with her husband, Harry. She had to cut the emotional apron strings.

Sometimes it's hard for parents to step back and not give advice and interfere. But throughout a marriage, partners must continue to refocus their lives on each other and give their relationship with each other a higher priority than other relationships. And it's not just in-law relationships! If you put your career, children, sports, hobbies, or whatever before your mate, nothing you can buy or give your mate will really satisfy.

Is there anything in your life you need to give a lower priority than your relationship with your mate? What about your job? Or your children? What about your hobbies or friends or television? Are you over-involved in community, church, or civic activities? We knew one husband who had a different function to attend every night of the week! Unless you are willing to make your relationship with your spouse a higher priority than other relationships and activities, you will not have a growing marriage.

Most would probably agree that the marriage relationship should be a top priority, but in days, hours, and minutes, sometimes it just doesn't work out that way—even when we try. Cindy and Doug have three active boys four years old and younger. Sometimes the stress of parenting gets to them. "We really try to make our relationship a priority," Cindy said. "Last week I went through the hassle of getting a sitter and we slipped away to a restaurant, but we just sat there and stared at each other. We were too exhausted even to talk!"

Love is a delicate balancing act. Some things we can control; other things we juggle. An excellent book to help you find balance (without adding more guilt) is *Boundaries* by Drs. Henry Cloud and John Townsend (Zondervan).

If we peel off the layers of activities and time commitments, what is underneath? Do you often have wistful thoughts about your mate? Do you use wisely the time you do have? We told Cindy and Doug that they probably needed to go somewhere and sleep instead of forcing tired conversation over a meal. We suggested that they try to get away for twenty-four hours and even offered to be the milk carrier for their baby. (Cindy was still nursing their baby, so we offered to "pick up" her milk and deliver!)

What about your situation? Are there things you need to give a lower priority so you can put your marriage first? For instance, in mapping out your schedule for the next several weeks, why not start with writing in date times for you and your mate? Then add discretionary things like golf, shopping, and community volunteer activities.

Commit to Grow Together

Building a high-priority marriage includes a lifelong commitment to grow and change together. Unless you are really committed to your marriage, it's easy to give up when problems come along; anyone who's been married for more than a few days knows that problems will surface. All marriages have problems, but the difference in those marriages that make it and those that don't is that the successful ones are committed to growing together and working to solve each problem that arises.

A commitment to growth goes beyond just sticking together. It's also a commitment to adapt to each other's changing needs. Elaine confided, "Sam and I have been married for only six years, yet we both have changed so much. If we change as much in the next six years, I'm afraid we'll grow apart. How can we make it over the long haul?"

Elaine's question is shared by many others. We told her, "to build a vibrant, long-term marriage requires a willingness to grow and adapt to each other's changing needs. In one sense, you continually adjust and change to maintain the same loving, alive relationship."

If we refuse to grow and change, we will only have a mediocre marriage. Adapting to each other requires self-sacrifice. It calls for thinking of the other person and looking for ways to grow with and adapt to each other's changing needs.

It means being each other's best friend—being that one person the other can always count on. What are you doing to adapt to your mate? Do you share common interests? While you benefit from your differences, you also benefit from shared activities. As you go through your ten dates, you will have opportunities to talk about things you would like to do together. In a growing, healthy marriage, partners are friends and continually seek to understand, adapt, and grow together.

Work at Staying Close

In a high-priority marriage, not only do spouses grow and adapt to each other, they also work at staying close. Unfortunately, many things tend to push us apart—like overcommitment or lack of sleep. We try to avoid negative situations as much as possible. For instance, when we find ourselves overcommitted once again, we try to pace ourselves and say "no" when we need to. When you have a choice to make, ask yourself, "Will this action or attitude bring us closer together, or will it put distance in our relationship?"

Working at staying close will help you build an intimate love relationship. In a healthy, alive marriage, partners complement each other and experience a unique oneness with each other through the sexual union. They are committed to growing in intimacy in all areas, enjoying one another completely. They stay close through focusing on helping each other. Any help we offer our mate helps our marriage partnership. Any pain, hurt, insult, any lack of support or faithfulness, any failure to help our spouse will reflect back on our marriage. We can be the most positive reinforcing person in our partner's life and our partner in ours if we are willing to follow these three principles of putting our marriage first, growing together, and staying close.

MARRIAGE IS A PARTNERSHIP

*W*hen the goal is to make marriage a priority, both partners must be willing to share the load, to build a partnership. We still are complete individuals; we still care about others, our careers, our family and friends, but we must continually choose to put our marriage first.

Where are you in this process? Are you the newlywed couple who is just beginning to learn how to make your marriage a priority? Good relationship habits formed now will enrich your marriage in the years ahead.

Are you in the energy crunch of parenting toddlers or adolescents? Remember, your kids will wait while you make your marriage a priority, but your marriage won't wait until your kids grow up!

Are you sandwiched between adult children, grandchildren, and aging parents? While this may be a difficult stage of family life, you need to continue to invest in your marriage. Wherever you are, there will always be "time grabbers" trying to rob your marriage of priority time.

Our marriages are never static; they are always changing—either growing or withering. When we neglect to make our marriage a priority, it's easy to get bored. Researchers tell us that the number-one cause of divorce today is failure to work on the marriage. Life is stressful. Sometimes life is just plain hard. But the hard times, as well as the good times, can cause us to cling to each other—if we take the time to grow together. So our challenge is to grab time for your marriage today. Make your marriage a high priority by having ten great dates! Now it's time for action. Now is the time to date your mate!

Turn to Date One in the Marriage Alive Dating Guide and get ready to have a high-priority marriage!

Date Two

Learning to Talk

An experiment was conducted to determine the average amount of conversation between a husband and wife in a typical week. The participants wore microphones that recorded every word spoken, from "Hi, I'm home" to "Where's the remote?" Would you believe the average communication time was only seventeen minutes a week![1]

What has happened to communication in marriage? Certainly none of us got married and then took a vow of silence. Why do we stop talking to the one we chose to spend the rest of our lives with? Harry and Liz Brown wondered too. At a Marriage Alive seminar Harry said in frustration, "I can talk to my dog—but not to my wife. I always know how my dog is going to respond—he constantly loves me, so I can tell him anything. Liz is a different story. I never know how she will react."

"Harry pats the dog and walks right by me," Liz said. "I feel closed out of his life; I feel helpless." She wasn't even getting her seventeen minutes.

THREE PATTERNS OF COMMUNICATION

If the Browns are going to grow and have an alive marriage, they need to learn how to communicate effectively with each other. A marriage relationship is only as intimate as the conversations you have with each other. Words can help to build an intimate relationship, or they can destroy the very foundations of your marriage. It's your choice. By understanding three patterns of communication, you can hone your communication skills and develop the habit of using the more helpful patterns.

Pattern One: Chatter

Chatter refers to surface conversations. "Did you sleep well?" "What do you want to eat for dinner tonight?" "Do you think it is going to rain today?" "I can't find the car keys. Have you seen them?" Chatter is part of healthy conversation; we use it every day. But when chatter becomes the predominant marital communication pattern, problems arise. Chatter is safe—no sparks fly—but if that is as deep as your communication goes, chatter is a shallow and lonely pattern.

Pattern Two: Confrontive

Authors and marriage specialists Drs. David and Vera Mace refer to the confrontive pattern of communication as "the communication style with the sting in the tail!" It hurts. In the confrontive pattern, we use "you" statements and ask "why" questions, like "Why did you do that?" or "Why don't you think before you speak?" We attack the other person without even realizing what we're doing.[2]

The problem arises when this attacking style of communication becomes a pattern. Our goal whenever we get into the confrontive mode (and at times we all will) is to get out of it as quickly as we can! One way to get out of it is simply to say, "My, that sounded like the confrontive style to me!" This alerts the other that whether it was intended or not, you felt attacked. A wise partner will accept this reminder and back off.

In a recent seminar, when we discussed the confrontive pattern, we brainstormed different signals we could use to alert our partner.

One participant suggested using the phrase "Red light!" when one of you feels confronted. That afternoon during a seminar break, one of the seminar couples, Ben and Lillian, took a drive along the California coastline. Lillian was behind the wheel. Romance, laughter, and fun were in the air when, out of the blue, Ben said, "Red light."

"What?" said Lillian, unaware of saying anything confrontive.

"Red light!" said Ben, with more urgency.

Puzzled, Lillian looked up just in time to understand what Ben meant. She was about to run a red light at a major intersection! So if you use "red light" as your cue, find another signal for times you are driving!

To log less time in the confrontive pattern of communication, the Maces suggest making a contract never to attack each other intentionally. From time to time we still attack, but our attacks are unplanned! We have agreed to two simple principles:

1. We will not intentionally attack each other.
2. We will not defend ourselves. On those occasions when we slip and attack the other, the one who feels attacked can diffuse the confrontation by choosing to take the higher road and resisting the desire to justify or defend his or her position.

Our agreement helps us move on to a more helpful pattern of communication and one that can enrich and deepen our relationship.

Pattern Three: Companionate

The companionate pattern of communication is the "meat and potatoes" communication pattern for growing, healthy, alive marriages. With it, we can deepen our marital bonds, become intimate, close companions, and resolve our differences.

Companionate communication begins with a willingness to share our true self with our mate—to make ourselves vulnerable by letting the other know our most intimate thoughts and feelings. Our contract not to attack each other or to defend ourselves allows us to share our true feelings. We know the other will handle our feelings with tenderness, will not defend or justify him or herself, and will not attack when we make ourselves vulnerable. This opens the door for truly intimate conversations. Sharing our feelings on a deeper level helps build a strong communication system that enables us to handle problems when they come along.

HOW TO EXPRESS FEELINGS — BOTH POSITIVE AND NEGATIVE

*W*e would like to suggest a simple formula for expressing your feelings. We have used it for many years with each other, our children, and others. It is clear, simple, and nonthreatening when used with the right attitude.

"Let me tell you how I feel."[3]

The first part of the formula is to state clearly, directly, and lovingly, "Let me tell you how I feel. I feel ..." (fill in with a word that describes how you feel—*frustrated, angry, alone, hurt, disappointed, anxious, happy, joyful,* and so forth). Express your inward feelings and emotions, and avoid attacking the other person.

Don't confuse "I feel" with "I think." If you can substitute "I think" for "I feel," then it is not a feeling. For instance, "I feel that you hurt me!" expresses a thought and judgment. It is the confrontive style of communication in disguise. Much better would be to direct the statement toward yourself and say, "I feel hurt when this happens." You can also state your feelings by using the words, "I am," as in "I am hurt when this happens."

Author Gary Smalley gave a great suggestion in one of his seminars we attended several years ago. He suggested painting a picture that will help your mate understand your feelings. For instance, "Honey, remember when you worked so long and hard on that proposal and took it in to your boss, only to have him toss it aside and ignore what you had carefully prepared? Well, that's how I felt when I spent hours researching possibilities for our vacation, and you didn't want to talk about it." Bam! Your mate is reliving a feeling he or she has experienced and can now identify with your feelings.

Remember, you want to express inward feelings and emotions that reflect back on you and avoid attacking the other person. Feelings are neither right nor wrong; they simply are—but it's valuable to know how your mate feels. This leads to the second part of the feelings formula.

"Now tell me how you feel."

After you have stated clearly and lovingly how you feel, say, "Now tell me how you feel." Then be prepared to listen. Don't judge your mate's feelings. Remember they are neither right nor wrong!

"Wait a minute," interrupted Randy, a seminar participant. "How can you say feelings are neither right nor wrong? Some feelings are just plain sinful!"

A great discussion followed on the differences between how we feel and how we act and between what is a thought and what is a true feeling. "For example," Randy continued, "anyone can easily get off the hook by saying, 'I don't feel like going to work'; 'I don't feel like being a thoughtful spouse'; or 'I feel like having an affair.'"

Before we could respond, another participant spoke up: "We may feel a certain way, but that's not an excuse for doing or not doing what is right. I wouldn't have my job very long if I told my boss, 'I don't feel like coming to work today.'"

Another picked up the discussion: "I agree, but maybe the statement 'I don't feel like going to work' is not the *real* feeling or issue. Maybe you really feel worn out, taken advantage of, or bored with the job."

"Or," another added, "maybe the statement 'I feel like having an affair' is really saying on a deeper level, 'I'm bored with my marriage; I feel disconnected from my mate; I want more romance and excitement.'"

Now we were getting down to the real feelings.

Feelings are fragile, and we must handle them with care. But if we can get to the real issue through sharing our feelings, we can attack the problem instead of each other and at the same time strengthen our own marriage.

NO FEELINGS VOCABULARY!

*T*he couples in that seminar were beginning to get the picture when James, a middle-aged husband, said, "This all sounds great, but I couldn't say how I felt if I wanted to—I just don't have the words! My father said only three words, and none had anything to do with how he felt, and me, well, I'm a chip off the old block."

To help James venture into the world of feelings, we brainstormed words we could use to express our feelings. If you, like James, have difficulty expressing feelings, maybe our list will help you get started.

I feel . . .

hurt	angry	frustrated
happy	threatened	lonely
confused	inspired	stressed
loved	depressed	confident
excited	anxious	proud
belittled	joyful	used
peaceful	attacked	energetic
irritated	sad	helpless
content	enlightened	responsible
overwhelmed	encouraged	remorseful
left out	broken	sick
envious	trapped	stifled
squelched	tense	betrayed
nervous	relaxed	silly

grateful	abused	scared
perplexed	misunderstood	alone
pressured	burdened	afraid
optimistic	pessimistic	enthusiastic
crushed	numb	bored
discouraged	ignored	pleased
uneasy	deprived	embarrassed

How comfortable are you with words like those above? Are you willing to try the feelings formula? Are there areas you hesitate to discuss with your spouse? It may help to write down how you feel about an issue. Try using the feelings formula and, making sure you are stating your true feelings without attacking or blaming your mate, tell your mate how you feel (or let your mate read what you wrote) and ask for his or her feelings in response. As your mate speaks, seek to understand how he or she really feels about this issue.

For example, maybe you are concerned that you are both abusing your credit cards. You fear that financial troubles are in your future and want to talk about it and find a solution now. Remember, the overused credit cards and your fear of financial trouble are the issues you want to attack. You could write something like, "I'm anxious and fearful when we max out our credit cards and have no plan for how we can pay them off." However you word it, attack the problem, not each other!

LISTEN, DON'T ATTACK!

Why is it so hard to listen? Could it be that instead of really listening, we are thinking about what we want to say when our spouse stops talking? Listening is more than politely waiting for your turn to talk.

For years we had on our refrigerator door a card that read, "Listen, don't react!" But at times we still reverse it. We react and don't listen! Not only do we need to practice listening, we need to be aware of the total message. It's much more than the words.

LISTEN FOR THE TOTAL MESSAGE

It is not enough just to hear words. We need to hear the total message. A few years ago Kodak did a study to determine what makes up "the total message" in communication.[4] These are the results:

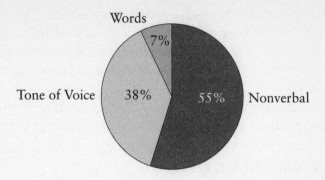

1. Our nonverbal communication accounts for 55 percent of the total message. This includes shrugs, stares, and glares. (We all know the "look"!) Or the lack of any interest at all. Picture one mate trying to talk while the other's attention is glued to the television or paper. Have you ever agreed with your mate verbally but given another message with a look of disgust on your face? There is no colder place to be than with a couple who are using the "right" words to gloss over bitterness, anger, and hostility.

2. Tone of voice accounts for 38 percent of the total message. This includes the sighs and nagging tones that creep into our conversations. Have you ever said, "Okay," when it really wasn't okay? Your tone of voice can send a completely different message.

3. The words actually spoken make up only 7 percent of the total message. Next time you talk to your mate, be aware that your words are only a very small part of the true message.

TOO HARD?

One Marriage Alive participant claimed, "It's just too hard. I've been 'me' for fifty years, and I'm not going to change now. Besides, this seems fake and unnatural to me." Maybe you feel this way too.

We understand. It wasn't easy for us either. Clear communication is hard work! It's hard to let the other know how you really feel. Just how will he or she use that information? At first when we tried to express our true feelings, it was easier for Claudia than for Dave. When

Claudia said how she felt, Dave would counter with, "Why do you feel that way?" or "No one in their right mind should feel that way!" We had to remember that feelings are neither right nor wrong, but knowing how your mate feels is vital to developing a communication system that works.

Even marriage experts don't always "say it right." For instance, we remember using all three patterns of communication in one day.

THE STRAWBERRY PATCH

*I*t was one of the two Saturdays each summer that Dave lavishes his attention on our otherwise neglected yard. Dave does not enjoy yard work, but two or three times each summer he gets out there and gives it his 200 percent. At breakfast, as we discussed the day, we used the Chatter pattern of communication. Claudia spent the day lying low in the office. (She didn't want to sidetrack the gardener and had a writing deadline to meet.) Since we were being so productive, we both felt good about the day.

Late that afternoon, Dave dragged into the house—dirty, tired, sore muscles, and all—but he had "done the yard!" and wanted to show off his accomplishments. So together we went outside to take a yard tour.

Everything looked transformed! Claudia was thrilled—until she came around the house to her strawberry patch. This was the year the strawberries were really going to produce, and she could already envision strawberries on ice cream, strawberries on cereal, and strawberries on shortcake!

As she looked at what was supposed to be her strawberry patch, she exploded in the confrontive style of communication. "Why did you do that?" Dave had inadvertently pulled up all the cultivated plants and had left the wild strawberry plants that needed removing! "Dave, you've ruined my strawberries! How could you do that to me—after the hours of work I've put in! I can't believe you didn't at least ask what to pull!" Claudia's anger was vented, and Dave secretly wished he had cemented the whole yard the year before. The confrontive pattern was alive and well. How could we get out of this mess?

We knew we couldn't solve the problem until we calmed down. Both of us had said things we regretted. It was time for damage control. "Dave," Claudia began, "I didn't mean to attack you. I just feel so disappointed that my strawberries are gone. I worked hard on them, and this is so frustrating to me!"

Dave responded, "I feel frustrated too. I spent the whole day in the yard, my body hurts, I'm tired, and now I find out I did it wrong. It's just that the wild strawberries actually had little red berries on them. I assumed they were real strawberries! I'm really sorry!"

Slowly, we were beginning to calm down—moving into the companionate pattern of communication. About that time we eyed the strawberry victims. The cultured plants were in a heap in the driveway. They were the problem. So we began to focus on them. As we began to think creatively together, we decided to try to replant them. Clearing out the wild plants gave us more room to replant the real strawberries. Before dark, Claudia's strawberries were replanted, and our relationship was restored. Plus, the strawberries lived. And we did have strawberries on ice cream, cereal, and shortcake! It takes determination and effort and courage to develop the skill of companionate communication. But take it from us, it's worth all the effort! In the next chapter you will see how developing the companionate communication pattern can help you resolve honest conflict.

Now, turn to Date Two in the Dating Guide and get ready to listen, to talk, and to have some fun.

Date Three

Resolving Honest Conflict

*W*e knew that this Marriage Alive seminar was going to be tough when one participant said at the beginning of the session on conflict, "We have no conflict in our marriage because I'm always right!"

Another added, "All my wife has to do is tell me her problem, and I'll fix it!" The look from his wife made her nonverbal message very clear: "Just try to fix my problem!"

No one gets married to add conflict to life. Quite the contrary. Romantic love blocks thoughts of future conflict. That's one reason it's difficult to teach engaged couples how to resolve conflict. They know *they* are the exception. Once married, however, to survive you've got to learn how to deal with your differences—including how to handle conflict and anger—or your marriage will self-destruct. Fortunately, learning how to resolve conflict and process anger is a skill we can all develop.

Dr. David Mace says in *Love and Anger in Marriage* that the biggest problem in marriage is not lack of communication, but the inability to handle and process anger. Look at the diagram below.

THE LOVE-ANGER CYCLE[1]

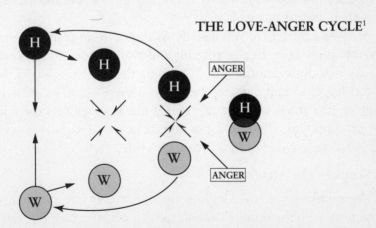

39

H represents the husband, and W represents the wife. When couples are dating before marriage, they are on the left side of the chart. They have a lot of space in their relationship. They are not together continually, but they want to be! After marriage, with less space, they run into more opportunities for disagreements and for sparks to fly. The goal is to resolve the conflict causing the anger and to break through to the right side of the diagram to intimacy. But often the couple does not resolve the conflict and each pulls back to the left side, giving one another more space. As couples repeat this love-anger cycle, walls begin to grow. The list of things a couple doesn't talk about grows as well, and intimacy in marriage is just a pipe dream.

Where are you on this chart? Perhaps you are caught in the love-anger cycle and would like to get out of it. You can break out of this cycle and move toward intimacy if you are willing to take the risk and work at resolving the conflict causing the anger. To begin, look at how you presently handle conflict.

HOW DO YOU HANDLE CONFLICT?

The ways we handle conflict can be compared to certain characteristics of some of the members of the animal kingdom. Do you see yourself in these inappropriate methods?[2]

The Turtle—The Withdrawer

Dave is the turtle in our family. When faced with conflict, his normal reaction is to withdraw. He just pulls his head inside his hard shell for the duration. Claudia, who occasionally likes an argument, can beat on his shell, but to no avail.

Are you a turtle? Do you usually withdraw from conflict? You may withdraw physically, like getting up and walking out of the room, or you may withdraw emotionally, by turning the other person off. Maybe you feel hopeless and defeated before you even begin, so why discuss it? Let us give you a word of caution: Withdrawing hurts the relationship, prevents your finding a possible solution, and moves you very quickly to the left side of the love-anger cycle.

The Skunk—The Attacker

The skunk sprays when he is being attacked or feels threatened. Do you identify with the skunk? Do you spray a verbal attack on your mate when he or she doesn't meet your expectations or when you feel your sense of security is being threatened? Many "skunks" are masters of sarcasm and put-downs. They use verbal skills to make the other person look bad rather than deal with any of their own shortcomings.

Claudia is a skunk. Her natural tendency is to attack and make Dave stink. She would rather focus on what he did or didn't do and avoid any responsibility on her part.

Over the years of leading Marriage Alive seminars, we've met many turtles who are married to skunks. We've even observed a new breed—the *skurtle*. The skurtle, a combination of the skunk and the turtle, handles conflict by attacking the other person and then retreating into his or her shell!

The Chameleon—The Yielder

The chameleon turns colors to blend into the environment, thus avoiding conflict. He agrees with whatever opinions are being expressed. When he is with a quiet group, he is quiet too. When he is with a loud group, he becomes loud. His desire to fit in and be accepted prevents him from expressing his real opinion, so when he meets conflict, he'll go along with the crowd.

Often this is the mate who leaves a marriage after thirty years of "giving in." No one can understand what triggered his or her departure, because he or she always adapted so convincingly. But everyone has a limit—like a balloon that stretches and stretches and then suddenly pops.

The Owl—The Intellectualizer

The owl, like the turtle, avoids conflict, but uses different methods. He intellectualizes; his motto is "Avoid feelings at all cost!" The owl gladly discusses an issue on an intellectual level but has no feelings from his cranium down. He deals with facts, facts, and facts.

Marc was an owl. When his wife, Wendy, forgot to take the videos back to the video rental store because she was comforting a friend whose husband was critially ill, he just couldn't understand. It's so simple. Just take the videos back and you will avoid the late charge!

The Gorilla—The Winner

The gorilla has to win at all costs. His favorite weapons are manipulation and intimidation. Underneath his tough skin is a person who may be very insecure and wants to look good no matter what the cost. He keeps mental files of old grudges, hurts, and wrongs to pull out and use at the appropriate time. He loves to tell you what is wrong with everything and why he is right!

We'll never forget the seminar where one participant, Bill, turned out to be the classic gorilla. Each session was a struggle because Bill constantly interrupted us to tell us what we were doing wrong—or how we could do it better "his way." He continually attacked and put down his wife. The solution came from among the participants. During a break, several husbands slipped away and came back with a huge bunch of bananas for Bill. He finally got the message! Did he make a drastic change for the better? Not really, but he worked on modifying his behavior.

WHAT'S YOUR STYLE?

Do you identify with any of our animal friends? You may identify with more than one because we may react to conflict in different ways at different times and with different issues. What issues keep coming up in your relationship? Sometimes we argue over insignificant things such as

- You like the house to be as warm as the tropics, and your mate would make a good Eskimo!
- You are Mr. Pro and are married to Mrs. Con (or vice versa).
- You like the toilet paper to unroll from the top, but your mate likes it to unroll from the bottom.
- Your middle name is Punctuality, but your mate's the Late Arriver.
- You like that homey, lived-in look, but your mate arranges the magazines on the table at forty-five degree angles.
- You are a precision toothpaste roller, but your mate's a creative squeezer.

If little things don't make sparks fly at your house, big issues such as finances, children, sex, in-laws, priorities, and time management can ignite conflict.

The key to resolving conflict isn't the issue you are arguing about. Instead, the key is developing a way to look at that issue from the same side. In *Fighting for Your Marriage*, authors and marital researchers Drs.

Howard Markman, Scott Stanley, and Susan Blumberg encourage couples to work at resolving conflict as a team. They write: "You have a choice when dealing with a problem. Either you will nurture a sense that you are working together against the problem, or you will operate as if you are working against each other."[3]

As we discussed in chapter 2, learning to express your true feelings and to understand your mate's feelings will facilitate good communication. Then you need to keep on talking until you both understand the issue and desire a solution—even if you have to give a little, or a lot. When you get to this point, conflict resolution is a piece of cake! First, let's evaluate how you are doing at expressing your feelings and discussing issues. Then we will give four simple steps for resolving conflict.

EVALUATING AND EXPRESSING OUR FEELINGS

*T*hink back to the last time you were angry. How did you feel? Did you feel misunderstood? Afraid? Frustrated? Let down? All alone?

What do you do when you become angry? During the first year of our marriage, Claudia got so angry that she threw Salvo soap at Dave. Salvo was soap in bullet form. (It's no longer available—we guess it was just too dangerous!) Here's the situation. On the weekends when we visited Claudia's parents, we brought along our dirty clothes to wash. On this particular weekend, Claudia was upset with Dave. She had washed all three loads of laundry, folded the first two loads, and ironed Dave's cotton shirts. All he was supposed to do was put the last load (our sheets) in the dryer, but laid-back Dave forgot. Here we were, ready to leave and where were our sheets? Still in the washer! Claudia, already feeling she was doing more than her share of work, skunked Dave! "Why couldn't you at least remember the sheets? Am I the only one who is responsible for the laundry? I need a break too!" Our agrument escalated, and before we knew it, Dave was dodging Salvo! His response? He simply pulled into his shell, and threw the wet sheets in our little VW bug. The drive back to Altanta was very quiet. We knew there must be a better way, but at that time we didn't know how to handle our anger appropriately.

As we said earlier the turtle withdraws; the skunk attacks; the chameleon yields; the owl intellectualizes; and the gorilla persists until he wins.

Years later Claudia wishes she could have acted less like a skunk and chosen from these more appropriate responses to anger:

- Put the "hot potato" down and let it cool.
- Identify confrontive communication and get out of it quickly.
- Stop the escalation of anger.
- Resolve the conflict together and move on into intimacy.

You can do all of the above. But first you need to process your anger. Remember the feelings formula from chapter 2? You can share negative feelings in a positive way if you have made a contract not to attack each other or defend yourself. Also, at the first sign of anger tell the other person that you are getting angry. Otherwise, one of you could be angry and the other wouldn't know it!

You might say, "Honey, I'm getting angry with you, but I have agreed not to attack you. Could we talk about what is causing my anger and see how we can work things out?" You are still taking ownership for your feelings and anger and not blaming or attacking the other person.

Wouldn't any spouse in his or her right mind respond positively? Once the anger is diffused, you can discuss whatever is causing the conflict. But until you process the anger, you can't resolve conflict. So we encourage you to make your own anger contract. We suggest actually signing a written contract with these three points:[4]

1. I will tell you when I am getting angry with you.
2. I will not vent my anger on you.
3. I will ask for your help in finding a solution for my anger.

Only when you first deal with your feelings can you deal effectively with the issue. By truly understanding how each feels about any given issue, you can talk about it, focus on the issue, and refrain from attacking or blaming each other. What a difference this makes when you get to the step of actually trying to find a solution!

STEPS FOR RESOLVING CONFLICT

Once you have expressed and understood your feelings, you can move on to the four steps for resolving conflict.[5] The first step is to agree on what the issue is and that you both want a solution. Write down the problem you want to resolve. In our Salvo War, the real issue wasn't the sheets but the unfair division of labor!

Step Two is to identify which one of you needs a solution and the other's contributions to the problem. Dave was perfectly happy with they way things were so it was Claudia who needed a solution. She wanted Dave's involvement and help!

Step Three is to brainstorm possible solutions and list them. If we had followed steps one and two, we would have short-circuited our attacks, and we could have brainstormed creative ways to solve our problem of wet sheets and division of labor.

Step Four is selecting a plan of action. From your list of solutions, choose one you both would like to try. If it works, great. If not, go back to your list and try another one.

THE THREE C'S[6]

*Y*ou may discover that most plans will involve some give and take. Basically there are three ways to reach a resolution. The Maces call them the three C's: Compromise, Capitulation, and Coexistence.

Compromise simply means we each give a little to find a solution that we both can live with. This is the way we find a solution to many of our differences. We have a continuing dialogue on snack foods. Dave likes the yummy, high-fat, high-cholesterol, high-taste treats. Claudia would rather have only carrots and celery. We compromise with pretzels, popcorn, and the occasional caloric and fat splurge. We also have vegetables and dip—but not every day. Snack food is not a major issue at our house, but like the remote and thermostat, it can become a chronic irritation.

The second C is Capitulation. We aren't talking about the army general forcing a surrender. Capitulation in conflict resolution is more like giving a gift of love. Some issues are more important to one person than to the other. So one way to resolve the conflict might be for the one who doesn't have as much at stake to capitulate and go along with the other. For example, when we remodeled our kitchen, Claudia picked out the blue paint sample she liked. Dave, convinced that it was purple instead of blue, couldn't imagine our walls that color. Since Claudia had the stronger feeling about the color of the walls and more expertise in decorating. Dave capitulated and went along with Claudia's choice. It ended up looking great—and blue!

Coexistence, the third practical way to find a solution, teaches us that we don't have to agree on everything. In some areas it's okay to agree to disagree. For instance, take food preferences. Dave likes beets, while Claudia doesn't even like to smell them! So imagine Dave's surprise when one summer Claudia took him on a tour of her vegetable garden and showed him the beets she was growing just for him! Later, she confessed that she thought she was planting radishes.

At different times and in different situations, we use all three C's. Maybe you have differing political views or like different styles of music. Remember, our goal is not to be alike; some differences add spice to our marriage. The problem arises when one of you continually gives in to the other or when you choose to coexist on everything or you use compromise as a means of "horse trading" and manipulation. Power plays and attempts to manipulate destroy the potential for love and closeness in a relationship. The key is being willing to keep talking and sharing your feelings until you both understand the issue and want to resolve it.

THE WAR OF THE TOWELS

*W*hile the steps of conflict resolution are simple, we repeat, do not use them until you are *sure* you have talked about all of your feelings, have identified the issue, and agree that you both want a solution. In one Marriage Alive seminar, we learned the hard way what happens when you try to resolve an issue before adequately discussing it.

Our seminar was running smoothly until we got to the steps for resolving honest conflict—then war erupted! After giving the participants the steps for resolving an issue, we chose what we thought was a fun, simple situation to illustrate how the steps worked. We started by defining the problem: "I don't like towels left on the bathroom floor."

If looks could kill, we were already in trouble. We also observed elbow nudging and whispered comments. We chose to ignore these hints that all was not well and proceeded to step two—identifying which one needed a solution and the other's contribution to the problem.

We arbitrarily said: "The wife has the need. The husband leaves wet towels on the floor." The "looks" told us we were about fifty percent correct. We figured, when all is silent, just move on to the next point. We were digging our grave and didn't even know it.

Step three was brainstorming possible solutions. A few humorists in the group helped us complete our list:

- Leave towel on floor
- Wife picks up towel
- Husband picks up towel
- Use disposable towels and throw away
- Don't use towels and drip dry
- Don't bathe
- Fold towel and put on rack

As we waited patiently for group consensus that the last alternative was best, war erupted. Rather than focus on the problem, the partners polarized, picked sides, and shot off verbal bullets. In this group, towels on the bathroom floor was a major emotional issue. It took us some time to get control of the group and call a truce.

What went wrong? They were attacking each other and not the problem. This often happens when we bypass adequately discussing our feelings and identifying the true issue. If you get to the steps of problem solving prematurely (and you will know you're there if you start arguing!), stop. Go back to the feelings formula. Stop trying to solve the issue until you are sure you both agree what the issue is and that you both really want a solution!

That's what we had to do with the war of the towels. The group returned to dialoguing and telling each other how they truly felt about the towel issue. As they defused negative emotions by sharing their feelings (without attacking the other's views), they could then focus on trying to understand each other. When they were finally committed to finding a solution everyone could live with, they went back to the steps of conflict resolution. This time it worked.

In step four we're looking for the best plan of action. What is the best answer to the towel dilemma? The first C, compromise, ended the war. The group agreed that each person should pick up his or her own towel and put the towel back on the rack or in the hamper. Problem solved. War ended.

While the war of the towels seemed to be a big issue with this group, it seems minor compared to other issues that couples face daily.

Do these principles apply to situations more serious than the war of the towels? Emphatically, yes. Consider a dilemma we faced.

THE UN-FUN DISCUSSION OF FUND-RAISING

Our magazine column on communication was finished and faxed. Then it happened. Claudia asked a simple question with no malice intended: "Dave, when are you going to raise funds for Marriage Alive?" This question brought up on Dave's mental computer all the fund-raising conversations of twenty years. Much of our work in marriage and family enrichment is fun, but fund-raising is at the bottom of the fun list! We had beaten this issue to death in many conversations, but that day its ugly head poked up again.

Could the authors follow their own advice? Not at the moment. Dave, feeling attacked, responded in kind. The turtle stonewalled the issue. Another quiet evening at the Arps. Well, not so quiet. Claudia's verbal attacks were definitely coming through loud and clear. "Well, I guess we should just go into another line of work," Claudia ranted, "something that doesn't involved fund-raising. You're never going to get around to it!"

Dave's response? Silence. This was simply maddening for Claudia! We were both totally frustrated! Do you ever get in those situations, where you feel you are going to scream if your spouse brings up an issue just one more time? That's how Dave felt about the fund-raising issue.

We all exchange negative feelings from time to time, but when we go too far in expressing negative feelings or do it over and over again, we may experience what psychologist Dr. John Gottman refers to as "system overload" or "feeling flooded." You feel overwhelmed and become defensive or as Dave did, just shut down. Men tend to be more reactive to stress and become flooded easier than women. This may explain why Dave and so many other men stonewall.[7]

How could we resolve this issue and solve it once and for all? Was there any hope for resolution? Not until we took our own suggestions. First, we had to cool off. Fund-raising was like a baked potato too hot to touch. We had to put our "hot potato" down and let it cool. If we go head-to-head in a heated confrontation, we lose perspective, attack each other, and generally make the situation worse. This conflict really caught us off guard—especially after we had spent the day writing about good communication.

"Cooling off" is not just a phrase. Dr. Gottman points out that there are also physical symptoms when you are flooded. You may find it hard to breathe. Or you may tend to hold your breath. Muscles may tense up, and the heart may beat faster. While women also experience the emotion of flooding, their bodies cool down and return to normal sooner than men's bodies do. So wives, give your husband plenty of time to cool down before resuming the discussion.[8]

While our potato was cooling and our common sense was returning, we both became fearful—if this doesn't work for us, why are we writing about it? While Dave felt flooded, Claudia felt misunderstood and alone. The fund-raising issue had been around for a long time, and we had resolved it before. Yet growth opportunities for Marriage Alive International brought new funding needs. Once we calmed down we decided to walk through the four steps of resolving conflict. Our steps for resolving the fund-raising issue looked something like this:

Step One: Define the problem.

Neither of us enjoys or is gifted in fund-raising, yet funds must be raised for the ongoing work of Marriage Alive.

Step Two: Identify which of you feels the great need for a solution and the other person's contribution to the problem.

We both needed a solution. Claudia possibly felt more insecure about the Marriage Alive financial situation than Dave did, but both admitted the need for a well-thought-through fund-raising plan. Both of us had contributed to the problem by doing very little to let others know of the need.

Step Three: Suggest alternate solutions.

Our list went something like this
1. Dave assumes full responsibility for fund-raising.
2. Claudia assumes full responsibility for fund-raising.
3. Cut back on existing programs.
4. Involve others in helping raise funds for Marriage Alive.

Step Four: Select a plan of action.

Compromise was a strategic part of our plan of action. Both of us had invested much in Marriage Alive and wanted to see our work grow. We needed to approach any possible solution as partners, yet neither of us had interest or expertise in fund-raising. It not only didn't make the top ten in our "I'd like most to do" list; it wasn't on our list at all! Here is our compromise agreement.

1. Claudia agreed to stop flooding Dave with comments about fund-raising. He could only handle just so much of her "helpful advice!" She agreed to help where she could. Specifically, she would help write and edit letters, stuff and stamp envelopes.

2. Dave agreed to acknowledge Claudia's feelings of fear and frustration, and to let her know he really *understood* how she felt. But if he didn't understand, he would try to understand, and he would willingly talk about their situation. He agreed to stop procrastinating and to do what he could do, rather than concentrating on what he couldn't do. He would work on improving communication with our board and with present contributors.

3. Both would monitor spending and look for ways to economize.

4. To supplement our weak areas we added to our board of directors a key husband-wife team who both have expertise in administration and fund-raising. As they give suggestions and advice, we follow up with action. We have learned an important principle—we do what we can, one thing at a time.

Is this issue resolved once and for all? No, but we are making progress—we are on the same side, and things are much more pleasant at the Arps.

EVERYBODY HAS PROBLEMS

As long as we are married or alive, we will face hard situations and have to make choices. The dullest marriages on earth are the ones where both spouses have decided to coexist and merely tolerate one another—no conflict but no intimacy either. Let us challenge you to process your anger, frustrations, and differences and strive for intimacy. Your marriage is worth it!

A WORD OF CAUTION

Choose your timing wisely. Avoid bringing up emotional issues late at night when you're tired or when you're hungry or already out of sorts. And remember, power plays destroy the relationship. Don't be like the seminar participant who thought he was always right. It's hard to work together on resolution; it's hard to resist using emotional blackmail. But it's worth the effort to achieve honest resolution. Your marriage will be stronger for it. And when it applies, remember our suggestion to look to the one with more expertise in an area.

There are times when Dave feels more strongly about an issue and Claudia agrees to go along with him. Other times when Claudia has felt strongly about a decision, Dave has capitulated. It's not always easy to discern what to do. At times, we have done our best to make the right decisions, yet experienced disastrous results. Do we give up on resolving conflict and seeking to make wise decisions? No! And neither should you.

What about when you reach a stalemate and you just can't seem to work things out? Remember, a professional counselor can give you short-term help. If you're going down a one-way street in the wrong direction, you don't need a pedestrian shouting to you that you're going the wrong way. What you really need is a friendly policeman to come along, stop the traffic, and help you get turned around. That's what a counselor can do for your marriage.

But in most instances, if you are willing to pull together, to attack the problem and not each other, to process anger and work together at finding a solution, you can find one. Then you can concentrate on how to be your mate's best encourager.

Now turn to the Dating Guide and begin planning for Date Three. You, too, can learn to use anger and conflict to build your relationship.

Date Four

Becoming an Encourager

We'll never forget the knock on our door late one winter night when we were living in Vienna, Austria. As we woke and groggily answered the door, we were surprised to see our friends from Warsaw, Poland.

This was December 1981—several years before the dissolution of the powerful Soviet Union. The Soviets were threatening to take over the Polish government, forcing officials to declare martial law to control a nervous citizenry and minimize rioting and political dissension. The newscasts were brimming with stories of unrest and tension: Poland was a country on the brink of disaster. Seeing Tom and Karen and their three small children at our door brought celebration and relief.

After they told us their story, we were doubly glad to have them safely in our home. "As we were leaving Warsaw," Karen told us, "we actually passed lines of Soviet tanks rumbling into the city. It was frightening!"

Tom continued. "We didn't know what the situation would be at the border into Austria. We had to wait hours, but here we are!"

Tom made a phone call and the next thing we knew, a reporter from a news service came to our door. Tom and Karen handed him what turned out to be one of the first videos to make it out of Poland—proof to the world of the turmoil and upheaval martial law had caused.

Tom and Karen were obviously distressed. Not only did they have to flee their home in fear for their personal safety, they had no idea if they would ever return to their home, work, and friends. Pulling a small trailer behind their car, Tom and Karen brought as many of their personal belongings as they could. Their immediate future was unclear.

Imagine being uprooted from your home and friends—not knowing when you might get to return—if ever! Add three small children, sickness, and other pressures. It wasn't long until our friends were near emotional bankruptcy. They needed time to think—time to regroup. After the holidays, we encouraged them to take a few days without their children and go away.

Things looked bleak as they drove away that cold, January morning. Karen was tired, depressed, and feeling guilty about leaving their children. An hour later, they stopped for lunch, and for the next thirty minutes, Tom told Karen the things he appreciated and admired about her. He liked the way she was always there for him, her sense of humor, her sensitivity to the children's needs, her vital faith in God, her pioneer spirit (they had been living in Eastern Europe since the seventies, before the wall came down). Small things, big things, insignificant things—on and on he went, describing what he appreciated about her. What a significant difference that thirty minutes made in Karen's outlook on life; it certainly set the stage for a great getaway. From the beginning of their time away, Karen knew that she was loved, admired, and respected. During their week together, Karen wrote: "It's amazing how things come into focus when we take the time to be alone and encourage one another. We've had so much fun, but now we're ready to come home, even though we still must face unsolved problems and an uncertain future."

Several months later, they were able to return to their home in Warsaw, and the next year we led a Marriage Alive seminar for their group there.

THE OTHER SIDE OF THE COIN

The results could have been quite different if Tom had said instead, "Honey, you've just got to get control of yourself. Can't you stop crying? You're not coping well at all. This just isn't like you. Your attitude is having a negative effect on our children and even on me! If you tried harder, I know you could control your emotions." The week would have been a first-class disaster, and Karen would have been even more depressed. To tear down your spouse is one of the most cruel and unloving things you can do—it attacks the very core of the marriage relationship.

We desperately need to encourage and affirm each other. If we don't, who will? Our bosses and coworkers? Don't count on it! Our children and teenagers? Ridiculous! How many children walk in and say, "Mom and Dad, I want to express my appreciation to you for your consistent discipline and for refusing to let me do certain things I want to do because you know they are not in my best interest"?

Will our friends build us up? If we're fortunate they might, but we can't count on it. Our mates need our encouragement. You can positively influence your mate if you choose to build up instead of tear down. Here are three tips to get you started: Look for the positive, develop a sense of humor, and give honest praise.

Look for the Positive

Before marriage it's easy to see the positive. But once we marry, our rose-colored glasses tend to fade. Did you, like us, discover that the person you thought was just about perfect also had some irritating habits? The reality of living together creates tension, and it's easy to focus on the negative instead of the positive. Why does this happen? Look at the box below.

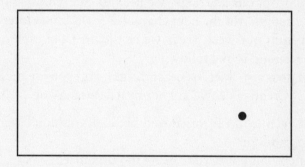

Where did your eyes immediately focus? On the small, dark spot? We tend to ignore all the light areas and see only the dark spot. In the same way, we have a tendency to concentrate on our mate's faults or weak areas. Why? Could it be that our own insecurities are showing?

It's hard to build up the other person when you feel insecure. If you are wrestling with personal problems, one of the most healthy things you can do to enrich your marriage is to get help for yourself from a counselor or a psychologist.

But for many of us, we simply need to refocus, to look for the positive. One wife in a Marriage Alive seminar confided, "With my husband, I tend to focus on the negative and concentrate on his weaknesses. I ignore the positive things about him. Now I'm beginning to realize that all relationships are fluid. They don't stand still. I want our marriage to move forward and grow. Starting right now I'm committing each day to look for ways to affirm my husband."

Johann Wolfgang von Goethe, the great German poet and philosopher, said, "If you treat a man as he is, he will stay as he is. If you treat him as if he were what he ought to be and could be, he will become that bigger and better man." Begin to look at your mate through Goethe's eyes. Maybe your spouse is in the process of taking a risk. Perhaps he or she is learning a new skill or even making a career change. Why not acknowledge and affirm your mate's strengths and his or her desire to grow and change? Taking the following steps will help you focus on the positive.

Concentrate on Each Other's Strengths

All of us have strengths and weaknesses. Strengths and weaknesses assure us of neither success nor failure. They are merely the setting where we play out our marriage. We need to let each other operate out of areas of strength. (In the next chapter we will look closer at how to do this.) Even in our weak areas we can learn from each other. How would you respond to the following?

Your mate is a stickler for organization, and you are the epitome of the maxim, "Creative people are not neat." Would you

- Not even try to be organized because you don't want to compete and lose?
- Criticize him or her for being too organized?
- Appreciate his or her gift of organization, verbally express that appreciation, and try to learn from your mate in this area?

Consider another situation: You love being a hermit, but your mate is a gifted conversationalist. How do you respond? Would you

- Criticize your mate for being too talkative?
- Send your mate as your representative to all social functions?
- Appreciate his or her natural talent in this area, verbalize your appreciation, and benefit from your mate's insights?

Every day we make choices to benefit from or be threatened by our mate's strengths. Do you appreciate the strengths your mate brings to your marriage partnership?

If so, it will help you through the hard times. We found that when we affirmed each other's strengths, some of our roughest times became positive ones.

The year before we began to work full-time in marriage and family enrichment was a rough year. The whole year was consumed with meetings, proposals, deadlines, delays, and more delays. Our days and nights were so stressful that many times we were ready to give up. For each three steps forward, we seemed to take two steps back. If we had not encouraged each other, we don't think we would have made it through the year.

Dave encouraged Claudia's creativity and organizational ability that helped us get our proposals formulated. Claudia affirmed Dave's enthusiasm in promoting our proposals to our parent organization and to funders. Claudia's discipline and drive kept us and our dream going, but when she became discouraged, Dave's deliberate, methodical consistency gave stability and helped us hang on until we got the go-ahead from our parent organization to branch out. Alone, either of us would have given up. Make your goal cooperation, not competition.

Track Your Positives and Negatives

Dr. Gottman in his book, *Why Marriages Succeed or Fail,* says, "You must have at least five times as many positive as negative moments together if your marriage is to be stable."[1] Observe your interactions with your spouse. Too often in marriage, the ratio of positive to negative is one to five; not five to one. What would your ratio be?

For the next twenty-four hours, keep track of the number of positive to negative things you say to your spouse. Remember that five to one is just staying even. Seven to one is a more healthy ratio.

Make a Positive List

When we think negatively, it's easy to express our negative thoughts, but when we do have positive, tender thoughts, often we keep them to ourselves. Positive thoughts are worth developing and worth expressing! However, stable habits take time and persistence to develop, so be prepared to persevere. Begin by making your own list of what you appreciate about your spouse. Then each day tell your mate one reason you would marry him or her all over again.

When you feel yourself moving into a negative thinking pattern, pull out your list and dwell on your mate's positive qualities. Keep on turning those positive thoughts into verbal affirmation. Think of it as a positive verbal recycle bin. Develop the habit of praising each other.

Give Honest Praise

The word *praise* comes from a Latin word for "worth," indicating a vital connection between the two. When we praise someone we value him or her. Descriptive verbs for *praise* are *commend* and *compliment*. Antonyms for *praise* are *blame* and *condemn*. It's easy to see which actions will build up and encourage! Let us add our own definition of praise:

Praise is describing what you appreciate.

Here are some practical tips for praising one another:

Be Specific

For example:

"I appreciate your initiative and creativity in our sexual relationship."

"I appreciate your thoughtfulness in calling me when you're going to be late."

"I like the way you listen to me when I tell you what's on my heart."

Describe—don't compare. Comparison can lead to trouble. For example, you might say to your spouse, "You are the best kisser in the whole world!" This could cause your spouse to wonder, "How would you know?" or "With whom are you comparing me?" It would be much better to say, "I like the way you kiss me."

Be Sincere

Flattery is counterfeit praise. It makes the recipient feel uncomfortable and manipulated. But it's fun to get an honest compliment. If we work hard to improve in an area, it's great to have a spouse notice.

A couple of years ago, motivated by a back injury, Claudia worked faithfully on her physical fitness. She lifted weights, exercised regularly, and walked fifteen-minute miles. While her major motivation was to have a healthy back, the side benefits included better muscle tone, less flab, and a lower number on the bathroom scales. As Dave began to notice these changes, Claudia appreciated his positive comments: "Hey, you look great in those slacks."

Be Vocal

We can have all kinds of nice thoughts about our mates, but power is only released when they are verbalized. Couples in a Marriage Alive Supper Club were studying how to encourage their spouses. Most admitted that they had not developed the habit of praise. They each agreed to give their mates five compliments during the next week. At the end of the week, one wife confided, "It felt strange to hear words of encouragement and praise come out of my mouth. But as I said them, it helped me see my husband in a different light."

Think about today or yesterday. Did you criticize your mate? Were you generous with words of praise? Remember that praise is verbal, and then consider these ways to practice praise.

Be Creative

Use Written Praise. Don't overlook written praise. Consider leaving little notes and jingles around for your spouse to discover. It's fun to receive cards and letters. Our friend Lucy, who has been married more years than we have, frequents card shops. If she finds a card she likes, but it doesn't say exactly what she wants, she edits it!

Look for ways you can be creative and abundant with your compliments. One Thanksgiving Claudia did an acrostic for Dave and for each of our children. Dave's read:

Dave is . . .
T ruthful
H elpful
A thletic
N ice
K ind
S uper
G reat Dad
I ntelligent
V ery creative lover
I nteresting
N ever a bore
G regarious

You can get a good buy on Valentine cards on February 15. One year we stocked up and hid them in various places all year long. When either one of us found one, we recycled it and hid it for the other to find.

Make a List. Make a list of things you appreciate about your mate. Our friend Joe made a list of thirty-one things he appreciated about his wife, Linda. He typed them, cut them up, folded them, put them in capsules, and gave them to Linda with the following prescription: "Take one a day for a month."

Give Coupons. Coupons are always fun to get. Include things such as

- One back rub with hot oil
- Breakfast in bed
- Dinner for two at your favorite restaurant
- A five-mile hike together.

Give a Gift for No Reason at All

Once, on a special promotional offer from a local department store, Dave purchased several small sample bottles of perfumes and lotions. He individually wrapped each one, and each evening he hid one under Claudia's pillow. The first night, she was surprised; the second night, she was more surprised; and the third and fourth nights, she even went to bed earlier.

A word of caution: If your mate reads this chapter and you begin to get little gifts, cards, and extra attention, enjoy it. Please don't say, "I know—it's just because you read that Arp book!" Instead, express your thanks and appreciation in your own creative way and be thankful for such a thoughtful partner. And then, learn to laugh together.

DEVELOP A SENSE OF HUMOR

A first cousin to encouragement is laughter. There are times in life when you can either laugh or cry. We try to choose laughter. Laughter dispels tension. It's good for your physical health, and it's definitely good for the health of your marriage.

When we laugh together, we seem to be more affirming. When we're under stress, we benefit from trying to find some way to lighten things up. Dan and Laura, like many other couples, have told us about the fun of pet ownership and how pets can relieve tension. Here's their story:

The pressure of med school, work, and other responsibilities were taking their toll. After a long day at work, Laura walked into their small apartment and found all three cats wearing ties! Dan, in an attempt to make Laura laugh, had tied his ties around the necks of their three cats. (It worked.)

We all have difficult situations in our lives. If we can step back, not take ourselves so seriously, and find something to laugh about, as Dan and Laura did, we can keep our relationship on a more positive track.

Helps for Developing a Better Sense of Humor

If laughter doesn't come naturally for you, here are some pointers that may help you become more jovial.

Give Yourself Permission to Be Less Than Perfect. No one is perfect. Not you nor your spouse! When you don't take yourself so seriously, you can relax, and it is easier to laugh and see the lighter side of life. If joking comes naturally in your relationship, consider yourself fortunate. But there is a fine line between jokes and put-downs. Laugh *with* your mate but only *at* yourself.

Cultivate Humor. We place cartoons and jokes on our refrigerator door and try to look for the humor in each situation, especially in irritating ones. Recently, as we sat in the Minneapolis airport waiting for our third canceled flight to be rescheduled, Dave looked at Claudia and said, "My, isn't it fun to be in the jet set?" Then we observed other passengers as the airline representative announced "mechanical difficulties" with the plane we were about to board. Looking around at all the disgruntled passengers, Claudia said, "This has to be the life of the rich and famous." Once again, humor came to our rescue. Some of our sources of humor are

- The cartoon section in our daily newspaper;
- Joke books and other humorous writings;
- Conversations from friends and business associates;
- Funny movies such as *Father of the Bride,* Parts I and II, or any classic comedy;
- Our e-mail pals.

Get Some Funny Friends. If you're both the sober type, find some funny couples to get to know. Years ago when we were leading a Marriage

Alive seminar in our home in Vienna, Austria, one couple attended who were just too serious. Both were opera singers, and both were introspective and intense. So we encouraged them to develop some friendships with couples who were not so serious. They took our advice. Having fun-loving friends helped them loosen up, laugh more, and enjoy life in a new way. Humor became one way they encouraged each other.

NOW IT'S YOUR TURN

*W*e have given you three tips for encouraging each other. We challenged you to look for the positive, to give sincere affirmation and praise, and to develop your sense of humor. Now it's your turn to put our advice into actions. We close this chapter with a challenge: Write a letter of encouragement to your spouse.

A favorite part of our Marriage Alive seminar is when we have the couples write a letter of affirmation to each other. Then, several months later, we drop their letters in the mail. But you don't have to wait for one of our seminars. Pen a letter to your partner right now and describe what you appreciate about him or her. If you mail it—especially if you send it to an office address—write "personal" on the envelope. (These letters have ended up on the company bulletin board!) Stamp it and drop it in the mail. Your partner just may write you back.

Rick and Sophie, participants in a recent seminar, told us how excited (and frustrated) they were when their letters arrived. Sophie told us, "We were delighted to get our letters, but the day they arrived was one of those really crazy days. We were both in the middle of big projects at work, and that was the week our three girls had what seemed like an extra twenty-five activities at school. (They needed a full-time chauffeur, and I was elected.) Rick and I decided not to open our letters but instead, to save them for a time when we could be alone. A few weeks later Rick's parents invited our daughters for the weekend. We saw this as a great opportunity for a getaway. I made reservations at a quaint bed and breakfast in the mountains. Fortunately, we remembered to bring our letters. The first night after a romantic dinner we opened and read our letters."

Rick added, "From that point the evening just got better."

Now it's up to you. Make your own positive list. Write your own letter. Look for humor. Encourage your spouse today. Your marriage will be better for it!

It's time for Date Four. Turn to your Dating Guide and get ready to encourage and to be encouraged!

Date Five

Finding Unity in Diversity

Two people can live together for many years and yet look at life from such different perspectives. Consider our friend who wrote us about her trip to Europe:

> In thinking of writing about our trip, I read over Ed's notes and thought we would combine our diaries, but now I wonder if we made the same trip. He remembers how far it is from Stockholm to wherever, what the money exchange was, what we had for breakfast, how many meals were on our own, and the address of every airline office in the four countries. In my diary I wrote about the things we did together—the places we visited and the interesting people we met. It really is a truism that opposites attract, and that God puts different people together to bring out the best in them. So if you want to know how far north or south we went, ask Ed. I have no idea!

Do you ever wonder if you're on the same trip as your mate? Opposites do attract; however, the very characteristic that attracted you to your mate—his or her easygoing nature, never in a hurry, always has time for people—may later be an irritation to you.

DISCOVERING OUR TEAM

We are very different from each other, and sometimes those differences create tension in our relationship. For the first eight years of our marriage we tried to change each other, and it just didn't work. Dave didn't understand why Claudia couldn't just "laugh things off" and not take life so seriously. Claudia wanted Dave to be more introspective and analytical.

And then we made a job change that required us to take a battery of psychological tests. We still remember the day we filled out those tests. Dave nonchalantly checked off his answers while watching a football game on television. Claudia carefully thought through each answer and cross-checked them for consistency.

The next week we were interviewed by Dr. Blaudau, a psychologist. He sat at his desk, looking at our test results. "Dave, here are your strong points." As he listed them, Dave began to feel better and better. He went on, "Now here are the areas in which you are weak." That wasn't nearly as enjoyable for Dave to hear, but the psychologist was right on target!

Then he went through the same procedure with Claudia, listing her strengths and weaknesses. Looking at both of us he said, "Dave and Claudia, here are the areas you agree on, and here are the areas in which you tend to have problems." His accuracy was uncanny—he didn't miss anything. Our respect for psychological tests went up about 300 percent. Then he gave us one of the most beneficial challenges of our lives: "You probably noticed, Dave, that your weak areas are Claudia's strengths, and Claudia, that your weak areas are Dave's strengths. If you will allow each other to operate in your areas of strengths and not be threatened by the other, you have the potential for building a great marriage partnership."

We would like to say that we went right out and applied his advice instantly—but it didn't happen quite like that. It's hard to admit that your weakness is your mate's strength and vice versa. It took time and practice, and at times it was awkward, but we took Dr. Blaudau's challenge seriously. We knew that if we could follow his advice, we would be a stronger team.

THE NEWSLETTER DILEMMA

One of our first attempts to apply this principle was in writing our newsletter. For years we have sent out a newsletter several times a year to those interested in our work. Over the years, the newsletter had become a real source of frustration and conflict. Writing newsletters was not Dave's favorite activity, yet for some reason (still unknown to us), Dave felt responsible for writing the letter. Claudia's gentle and not-so-gentle prodding did not help motivate Dave. However, once he finally sat down to write, he went on and on, ending up with a newsletter much too long and crowded with details.

Then Dave would give the letter to Claudia. A natural-born editor, she would offer her expertise: "It's much too long. Why did you include this part? Delete this. Here, I'll help you." At that point, Dave wanted only to be left alone. He knew Claudia enjoyed writing, but he wasn't benefiting from her strength.

After our interview with Dr. Blaudau, when it was time to write the newsletter, we reevaluated our strategy. If Claudia really enjoyed writing, why not switch roles? Together we planned the agenda for each letter. Then Claudia wrote the first draft. She thrives on feedback, so Dave would listen and give suggestions. Together we edited and reedited the letter. Since Dave likes details, he took over the responsibility for getting the letter printed, stuffing envelopes, stamping, and mailing. In the past he had been frustrated when Claudia purchased plain stamps. Now he was in control of stamp selection. In February, the stamp would say "love" or at least have a heart on it. Other times our stamps were color coordinated to go with our newsletter.

Our initial experiment to concentrate on each other's strengths had three results. First, our newsletters improved. Second, our relationship improved. And third, as we both used our strengths, we learned from each other. Over the years, Dave's writing has become clearer and more concise. Now we write books together. Claudia has become better with details, and if she's buying stamps, she may even look at the various commemorative ones.

PRACTICING BALANCE

*F*inances is an area where we try to balance our strengths and weaknesses. We've tried "Dave does it all" and "Claudia does it all" (the latter being a real disaster!). We didn't always agree about how to handle our finances and this led to tension and frustration. How did we change? First, we evaluated our strengths.

Dave has a mathematical engineering background—he's the detail-oriented person—so now he handles the basic accounting. Balancing the checkbooks, paying bills, and figuring our income tax returns is easy for him. This doesn't mean Claudia has nothing to say about our finances. She keeps up with the checks stubs and credit card receipts. Together we set our budget.

Claudia is the chief shopper. She can spot a bargain four stores away. She stretches our clothing and household dollars and does most of the grocery shopping. When Dave grocery shops, he is likely to come home with fifteen cans of soup and four pounds of pretzels but without the needed milk and bread.

Do we always agree about our finances? Of course not, but we have learned to communicate, compromise, and develop our own plan for how we earn, save, give, and spend our money. Working together has been a plus, especially in our finances.

UNDERSTAND YOUR STRENGTHS

Let us encourage you to assess your strengths and weaknesses and encourage each other to operate in areas of strength as much as possible. Batteries of psychological tests are not required to determine your basic strengths and weaknesses. However, if you have the opportunity to take them, we would encourage you to do so. We recommend several of the following psychological tests that can be administered by a therapist. Some even may be found as CD-ROM programs.

> The Myers-Briggs Type Indicator[1]
> The DiSC Test
> The tests from the book *Please Understand Me*
> Taylor-Johnson Temperament Analysis
> Marital Evaluation Checklist™

You can begin to identify your couple strengths. Your different strengths can help you balance each other—especially if you appreciate those differences and don't feel threatened by them. In areas where you have similar strengths, you may need to look for ways to work together harmoniously.

Think about ways you are different. Dave is laid-back and easygoing; he loves nighttime. Claudia is more activity- and time-oriented and loves rising even before the birds.

Think about ways you are alike. We have similar values. We're adventuresome and spontaneous and like to pioneer new things.

Can you think of ways your differences give balance to your marriage partnership? Are there areas where you are so similar that they might be liabilities? For instance, if neither of you is time-oriented, you may have to work hard to be punctual.

DISCOVERING YOUR COUPLE ASSETS

*T*o build a strong marriage we must learn how to benefit from the ways we are alike and the ways we are different. Consider several continuums that diagram a few of the many human polarities. As you look at each continuum, think about your own marriage. Both sides of each continuum have strengths and weaknesses, advantages and disadvantages. Which side you or your mate tends to be on is less important than understanding that people are different. Seeing where you are on each one will help you identify your assets and balance each other.

Some continuums have gender tendencies, but there are too many exceptions to place men on one side and women on the other. Also, from time to time, we may find ourselves at different places on these continuums. For example, in some groups you may be very extroverted and at other times quiet and introverted.

Even though human personality and relationships are incredibly complex, the following continuums can enhance your understanding of yourself, your mate, and your relationship. Think of each continuum as a seesaw and consider how you might balance each other. If you are both on the same side of the continuum, you will want to think about how you can compensate. The first continuum we will look at is Feelings/Facts.

Feelings-Oriented/Facts-Oriented

The feelings-oriented person tends to express feelings and emotions easily. He or she likes an open atmosphere, and if tension enters the relationship, the feelings-oriented person strives to clear the air. He or she desires to work through conflict and "not let the sun go down on" anger. This person needs feedback from the other. The feelings-oriented person is more relationship-oriented than facts-oriented.

The facts-oriented person speaks to express ideas and to communicate information more than to express feelings. He or she would rather not face unpleasant feelings and even becomes uncomfortable when emotional subjects arise, preferring peaceful coexistence to being confronted with emotions. This person is more goal-oriented than people-oriented. Our friend Ed is facts-oriented; he recalls the events of the trip, how much train tickets cost, and what time they arrived at the hotel. He references everything according to dry facts. His feelings-oriented wife remembers the joy she felt on walking through tulip fields or the trauma she endured trying to communicate with those who didn't speak English. For her, everything is framed in terms of her emotions at any given moment.

Suppose you are trying to reach a solution in a certain situation. One of you is more facts-oriented, the other is more feelings-oriented. Your different perspectives can be beneficial. If a decision is made purely on feelings, you may be in for trouble. On the other hand, if the decision is based entirely on cognitive information, you may be ignoring important input. Consider the example of a couple trying to choose between preschools for their three-year-old son. If the facts-oriented spouse alone made the decision, the most influential factors would likely be cost, proximity to home, compatibility of scheduling, and parent-teacher ratio. If the feelings-oriented spouse alone made the decision, the most influential factors would be more subjective: cheerful rooms, caring teachers, and children in a good mood. As you can see, all of these factors are relevant and necessary to making a thorough, balanced decision. One way of thinking is no more or less important than the other.

In your own relationship, what can help you achieve a balanced solution is to identify where you are both coming from. Stop right now and place yourself on this continuum. Then place your mate:

FEELINGS-ORIENTED   FACTS-ORIENTED

Do you balance each other? Dave is actually more feelings-oriented than Claudia, who tends to be more facts-oriented. Dave is sensitive to what's going on emotionally. It was easier for him to identify with our children—especially during their teens—while Claudia, with her cognitive approach, kept our ship moving forward. As parents and partners, we discovered we make better decisions together when we talk about both the emotions and facts. Both perspectives are important!

And what if you are on the same side of the continuum? For example, if you are both feelings-oriented, it's easy to get caught up in the excitement of the moment and overlook facts, like the couple who were shopping for a new car. They both got carried away and committed themselves to buying a new car on a used-car budget. They ignored their financial reality and ended up with large car payments that drained their limited budget. The next time they shop for a car, they will compensate for their weakness by doing their financial homework and deciding just how much they can spend before they hit the car lots.

On the other hand, if you are both facts-oriented, to make a decision based solely on facts is unwise. Many times there are negating emotional factors that need to be considered. Like in our car example, if only facts were considered, the couple may have purchased a car that they could afford but that they both hated to drive. So the next time you are faced with an important decision, discuss both the factual and emotional aspect of the issue. The first will be easy, but you may need to dig deeper to unearth the real emotional issues.

Private/Public

Another continuum is the private-public continuum. Privates like to be alone and to have time alone as a couple. They shy away from groups. Jay and Laura, both privates, recently attended our Marriage Alive seminar. They would love to live on a desert island and have little to do with others. Jay and Laura naturally protect their private times, but they could benefit from more involvement with others. We suggested joining a couple's group or a bowling league, or making a list of couples they would like to get to know and from time to time inviting a couple over for dinner or dessert.

Kelly and Mike are just the opposite. Both are publics. For them the more people the better. What's a vacation without friends along? They are energized by others, care deeply for others, and are involved in other people's lives. To achieve balance, Kelly and Mike need to plan time alone. Relationships are built in twos, and they need to be sure to plan enough "two" time to keep theirs healthy and growing.

Consider another couple. Carl and Sandy are at opposite ends of the continuum. Carl loves people and is continually inviting others to be a part of meals, vacations, trips—whatever. Sandy is more private and just wants to be with Carl. One of her favorite tricks is to kidnap Carl for an overnight getaway. Carl and Sandy work to find balance without one person overpowering the other by respecting each other's preferences and trying to have both types of interactions. Often, compromise helps them find balance between being too involved with others and no involvement at all. Where are you on this continuum?

PRIVATE   *PUBLIC*

If you are both privates or both publics, how can you compensate? At times when we get overinvolved with others, we have to regroup and plan time for us to be alone. Sometimes we look at the previous month's calendar to check how we're doing. This helps us plan for the next month.

Jay and Laura, the private couple from our seminar, now compensate by planning a couple of activities each month that include others. Last month they invited another couple to go "antiquing" together.

If you are opposites, how can you balance each other? For instance, each could plan one activity for the next few weeks. One might choose having friends over for dinner and the other might plan a date to go hiking on a lonely path.

Spontaneous/Planner

The spontaneous person is a first cousin to the feelings-oriented person. Life tends to just happen, unfettered by daily drudgery. Spontaneity is a way of life. As a result, the fun, exciting things get done. The more mundane side of life may be ignored—like menu planning, paying the bills, or housecleaning.

The planner likes structure and may be threatened by too much ambiguity. He or she is usually orderly and prefers to do things the same way time and time again. When interruptions occur, they are irritating if they prevent carrying out the daily plan. The planner needs a gentle push to expand his or her horizons.

By understanding yourself and your mate, you will be able to balance or compensate. For instance, the Arps are both spontaneous. Planning isn't exciting to us. Our Marriage Alive board of directors help us to focus. If left to our own devices, we like to do things on the spur of the moment. For us, setting objectives and detail planning is work. What about you? Where are you on this continuum?

SPONTANEOUS   *PLANNER*

If you are both spontaneous or both planners, how can you compensate? For instance, if you're both spontaneous, you could agree to check with each other before making any new commitments. Or if you're both planners, you could surprise your mate. Whatever you plan will be "planned" for you but will be spontaneous for your mate!

If you're opposites, how can you balance each other? Maybe the planner can defer to the spontaneous one, who says, "Why cook dinner tonight? Let's go out to eat." On the other hand, the spontaneous mate can agree to sit down and write out plans for the next week—"Next Friday we'll grill fish."

Active and Assertive /Laid-Back and Calm

We are so different on this continuum, that we had difficulty coming up with the terms to describe the diversity. We used to use the terms *active and fast* and *passive and slow*. We still aren't totally satisfied with our terms so we will try to describe what we mean. The active and assertive person tends to be goal-oriented. She is continually in motion. If those around her are not focused, she will happily help organize them. She has an abundance of ideas and the energy to put many into motion.

The laid-back and calm person is easy to be around. He is flexible and rarely gets rattled with life. The laid back person is not directive but exerts influence in other ways. He or she usually has a great listening ear, which is one reason many successful counselors have these attributes.

We are opposites. Claudia is the activist. Her definition of *boring* is "nothing to do." She doesn't like to take naps during the day—she might miss something. Dave would much rather just let life happen. He marches to a slower (but consistent) drummer. He is methodical and persistent and likes to cross all the t's and dot all the i's. On this continuum we benefit from each other's perspective and balance each other most of the time. But not all of the time! Like when Claudia gets superfocused on a project, she loses all track of time and can work nonstop for hours without a break. Dave will stop in the middle and take a fifteen-minute nap. It drives Claudia crazy. Or when we are trying to meet a deadline, Claudia will just hit the high points, and Dave gets upset because the details are missing!

Where do you fall on the following continuum?

ACTIVE AND ASSERTIVE   *LAID-BACK AND CALM*

If you are both active and assertive or both laid-back and calm, how can you compensate? Do you need to slow down or speed up? Do you need to cut your eighteen-hour day? If you're opposites, how can you balance each other? One way we balance each other is that Dave oversees details that demand consistency, like keeping up with our monthly obligations and managing our calendar, while Claudia moves us toward the big picture. She is the one to say, "Let's talk about our commitments for next year and how much traveling is reasonable." Dave, on the other hand, would say, "What about the details of today?" Dave also calms Claudia down when she gets hyper. At other times, Claudia motivates Dave to be a little more proactive.

Night Owl/Day Lark

Why do night owls marry day larks? It does help you survive the baby and teenage years. The night owl gets the night duty. Psychologists tell us we are born with an innate time orientation. What is yours? When is your most productive time of the day? Morning? Afternoon? Evening?

This continuum is the easiest to identify, but the hardest to balance. We first tried to change each other—it didn't work. But through the years we continue to work on harmonizing our clocks. Claudia's eyes automatically close about the time Dave's eyes pop open. His creative time is between 11:00 P.M. and 2:00 A.M., while Claudia's best time is early in the morning when Dave says, "No one in his right mind should ever get up that early!"

For us, one benefit to being opposites in this area is that it gives us space in our relationship. We work closely together for long hours. Sometimes Claudia likes to slip off to bed early, and at times Dave likes to delve into one of his midnight projects. What about you? Where do you fall on this continuum?

NIGHT OWL   *DAY LARK*

If you're both night owls or both day larks, how can you compensate? Many times your job or circumstance will do this for you. One of our night-owl friends is a surgeon who must arise early for surgery or to make hospital calls. His wife, also a night owl, tries to adjust her schedule. On vacations and off-the-job times they can stay up all night and sleep all day!

If you are opposites, how can you balance each other? When we had teenagers at home, it was easy for Dave to stay up until they arrived home. Claudia had morning duty when one of our boys needed an early morning school or sports trip send-off. It helped to acknowledge that we were different and that we weren't going to change the other—no matter how hard we tried.

Time-Oriented/Not Time-Oriented

Here is another continuum where the Arps are different. While we have found some benefits, we've also had to manage irritations. Claudia lives by the clock. Once her watch stopped about ten minutes before she was to leave for an appointment. She kept checking her watch and was so tied into her timepiece that she didn't realize for at least half an hour that it wasn't working.

Dave is the classic "non-timed" person. Like the popular author, Garrison Keillor, he's just "happy to be here." Time—what's that? Claudia's solution helped. She gave Dave a watch with three alarms, and at times he used all three. (But he had to remember why he set them!)

We learn from each other. Claudia has relaxed. Sometimes she is even ten minutes late. We both get to weddings on time, and Dave has graduated to a one-alarm watch. Where are you on this continuum?

TIME-ORIENTED   *NOT TIME-ORIENTED*

If you are both time-oriented or both not time-oriented, how can you compensate? Alarm clocks, alarm watches, notes to yourself, and an efficient secretary may help. Dave has a computer program that reminds him of things he needs to do. He even has a computer Post-It™ program! Since he is a detailed person, everything is on his computer. Rarely does he miss a deadline.

If you are opposites, how can you balance each other? For those really important occasions—like getting to media interviews on time—Dave works at being punctual. For other occasions that are not so important, Claudia tries to be more flexible.

WHAT ABOUT THE WEAKNESSES?

Our goal in marriage is not to be the same; we are very different. But we need to accept each other and benefit from our differing strengths and accept each other's differing weaknesses. If you find that one of you dominates on most of the continuums or concentrates on the other's weaknesses, it's time to reevaluate.

A seminar participant questioned us: "We've spent all this time looking at our strengths. When do we get to talk about the weaknesses of our spouses?" We used to do both, we explained, but one seminar experience made us reevaluate the benefits and liabilities of listing the weaknesses of the other. We'll never forget the time one husband approached us and said, "We've got a real problem in our marriage—I have all the strengths and my wife has no strengths, only weaknesses! Does this mean I'm supposed to do everything?"

Try as hard as we could, we were unsuccessful in helping him appreciate his wife's differences. He was on a negative track and refused to get off. Over the years, his wife had been beaten down, and her sense of self-worth was below zero. His negativeness had sapped the life from their marriage, and a weekend marriage seminar was inadequate to revitalize it.

Concentrating on our weaknesses is like poking an open sore. It doesn't bring healing. Over the past twenty years of leading our marriage enrichment seminars, we have observed that we help much more by concentrating on couples' strengths and helping them see their combined couple assets. When we do this, an amazing thing happens. We learn from each other.

A word of caution: A strength taken to an extreme can also be a weakness. We need to continually strive for balance. As a couple you have the wonderful opportunity to balance each other and combine your assets. But before you can clearly see and appreciate your couple assets, you may need to stop reacting inappropriately to your spouse.

DEALING WITH INAPPROPRIATE REACTIONS

*R*emember that we said that the very thing that attracted you to your mate before marriage, after marriage can become an irritation. What often happens when we see differences in our mate is we become irritated and then we react negatively.

Often we are so concerned with our spouse's different perspective that we cannot see our own inappropriate reaction. We suggest four steps for clearing our own vision.

Step One: List your spouse's differences that trigger your inappropriate responses. On a sheet of paper, make two columns. In the left column, list your mate's differences that trigger a reaction in you. In the right column, list your inappropriate responses to those differences. Perhaps your mate is not time-oriented and tends to be late. Do you assume automatically that he or she just doesn't care or is trying to annoy you by not being punctual? What is your response? Do you lecture, sigh, or give the silent treatment?

You may find that your responses are worse than your spouse's differences. If so, admit your negative attitude and burn or tear up the paper. Do not show it to your spouse; this exercise is for your eyes only! The following examples may help.

Differences in My Spouse That Trigger My Reactions	My Inappropriate Responses
1. Seldom home, wants to be with others	A. Neglect B. Nag C. Compare with others D. Criticize E. Be cool sexually
2. Spends money spontaneously, neglects bills	A. Reject B. Belittle C. Get angry—blow up D. Give the silent treatment

Step Two: Admit your inappropriate responses and attitudes. Remember, the emphasis here is to admit our inappropriate responses and attitudes, not identify or focus on our mate's differences. We must learn to take responsibility for our own actions and reactions before we can work on our relationships with others.

Step Three: Accept your mate with his or her strengths and weaknesses. Are you thankful for your spouse's strengths and weaknesses? Remember, your spouse's temperament can complement your own. It is impossible to change another person; we can only change ourselves. But when we concentrate on correcting our inappropriate responses and attitudes, wonderful things often happen. Others change in response to us. So don't waste time trying to change your spouse. Concentrate on being the person your mate needs.

Step Four: Ask your spouse's forgiveness for your past inappropriate responses. No relationship can thrive without forgiveness. No marriage is perfect; we all blow it from time to time. Relationships are like potted plants. The pot can be broken, but if the plant is repotted, if it is watered and given tender loving care, it will continue to grow and thrive. Forgiveness is a vital part of marriage. Without it, relationships die—like the potted plant left with its roots exposed. If your spouse asks you for forgiveness, give it. The director of a mental hospital said that half of his patients would be able to go home if they were forgiven and knew they were forgiven.

HOW TO SAY YOU'RE SORRY

*I*f you need to ask for forgiveness, do it in the right way. Focus on what you have done wrong, not on your spouse's shortcomings. For example, "Honey, I was wrong to nag you about being late to the restaurant. Will you forgive me?" Not: "I'm sorry I nagged you about being late, but you know you're wrong to always make us late!" Remember, you are pointing the finger at your inappropriate response. Don't use this moment as an opportunity to attack your spouse. If you attack your mate, you're attacking your own marriage team.

A word of caution: Let us repeat! If you find you need to go through these four steps, do not share your list with your spouse. This exercise is a private one, just for you, to deal with your inappropriate reaction to your spouse.

GET ON YOUR SPOUSE'S TEAM

*A*fter clearing your own vision, you will be able to see your spouse's strengths and weaknesses in a new way. Do you see ways your differences complement each other and give balance to your team? Together you can discover ways to compensate for areas in which you may be too much alike. Appreciate the uniqueness of your marriage team. You can build a wonderful partnership based on your combined strengths. That's what Harold and Joy discovered.

Several weeks after attending one of our Marriage Alive seminars, Joy told us, "In our twenty-eight years of marriage we had never heard about being a team. For us, this was revolutionary! We had become so bogged down in our individual roles—Harold is supposed to do this and I'm supposed to do that—that we missed benefiting from each other's strengths."

"In the seminar, you challenged us to concentrate on the positive and see our differences as assets," said Harold. "It's a totally new concept for us. After just a few weeks, it's made a big difference. We still have to work hard. It's easy to slip back into old patterns, but we're going to keep working on it and give it our best effort."

Like Harold and Joy, this may be a new concept to you. Let us encourage you to give it a try. Look for the hidden assets of your team. Be willing to continue to learn and grow together. You'll be amazed at the couple treasures you will discover! Amazingly, we discovered our greatest assets are our differences. What about you?

PSYCHOLOGIST REVISITED

*W*e began this chapter by telling you about our experience with Dr. Blaudau and that battery of psychological tests. Years later, we had the opportunity to retake them and to sit down again with the same psychologist. We were surprised and pleased to learn that we actually had learned from each other. Our weak areas were not as weak. We were a stronger team. We had proved it works! We challenge you to prove it for yourself. Work for unity in your diversity, and you, too, can be a strong marriage team. It will enrich your marriage—even your love life!

Turn to Date Five and get ready for a great date, finding unity in your diversity!

Date Six

Building a Creative Love Life

A young girl asked her grandmother, "Where did I come from?" The grandmother replied, "Honey, the stork brought you."

"But what about Mommy? Where did she come from?"

"We found her in the cabbage patch," answered her grandmother.

"What about you?" the granddaughter persisted.

"My parents found me behind the rosebush."

The next day at school the little girl reported to her class, "There has not been a normal birth in our family for three generations!"

What were your earliest impressions of sex? Did you, like this little girl, have some misconceptions? Do you remember the first time you became aware of the sexual dimension of life? What do you remember from your home of origin? Which of the following statements describe your childhood environment?

- My parents never or rarely used the "S" word.
- My parents openly talked about sex in a way that made it seem natural and positive.
- My parents rarely showed physical affection for each other or for me.
- I come from a family of huggers. My parents were very affectionate with each other and with me.
- I was uncomfortable asking my parents about sex. I basically learned about sex from other sources.
- I received mixed messages about sex. I wasn't sure if it was positive or negative.
- Based on my parents' attitudes, I looked forward to having a sexual relationship in marriage someday.

If your parents were comfortable with the "S" word and were open, honest, and positive in talking with you about sex, count yourself blessed. If, more typically, your parents choked on the word *sex* and left many unasked questions unanswered, you may have entered marriage with a confused picture of sex.

Thirty-four years ago, when we married, we had no premarital counseling in how to build a creative love life. There were few books dealing with the sexual relationship in marriage, so we entered marriage with little knowledge and several misconceptions. It was a subject most people were uncomfortable discussing. So we didn't realize that you have to work to develop a creative love life.

THE NEWLYWED GAME — LEARNING TO SAY THE "S" WORD

Do you remember your early marriage days? We were still in college and rice-and-beans poor. Once we realized we had to cultivate our love life, working on our sex life became our major form of entertainment. We decided to tackle building a fulfilling sexual relationship with all the gusto we could muster. We made some mutual commitments that helped us and can help you too—even if you have been married for a number of years.

We agreed to talk openly about our sex life. In some ways talking about sex was like learning a new language. We had to develop our "S"-word vocabulary, and then we had to use it! How would we know what the other liked unless we talked about it? We also talked about our fears and inhibitions. Claudia was much more inhibited than Dave, so a major part of "talking it out" was Dave's willingness to listen to Claudia.

We agreed to become explorers. Talking about sex wasn't enough. We needed to explore each other's bodies, discover what felt good, and what didn't feel good. Doesn't that sound simple? It wasn't. One thing that helped us was to plan times of "nondemand touching," exploring each other's body to see how good we can make the other feel. At these times sexual intercourse is not the goal. This helped us to relax, feel comfortable with each other, and eliminated the pressure of performance.

We became readers and learners. As we said earlier, there weren't many books dealing with how to have a great sex life, but we managed to find a few. The ones that had illustrations helped us to be brave enough to try different positions for lovemaking. Not all were successful, but along the way we began to learn what worked best for us.

We learned to be "other-centered." In our sexual relationship it's easy to become "me-centered" and lose our sensitivity to our partner. We forget that the best way to really please ourselves is to please our mate. When we focused on pleasing the other, we were less self-conscious. We tried to learn what turned each other on.

We found that Dave tended to be visual; when he thought about sex, physical intimacy was the goal. Claudia responded to tenderness and talk; when she thought about sex, her greatest desire was romance and emotional intimacy. Perhaps you will want to talk with each other about your love life. Do what you need to do to build a creative love life. It will enrich your marriage!

THE "S" WORD IN THE TWENTIES AND THIRTIES

About the time we began to really enjoy our love life, the kids started arriving, and we started dreaming about that day when there would be fewer interruptions and more energy. We handled our sex life and the first baby without too much stress, but when our second child arrived, things got complicated.

Psychologists tell us that the two times of greatest stress on a marriage are when you have toddlers and again when you have teens. If you have both, you have an extra challenge! For us, the most difficult time was when we had three children ages five and under. Dave, the night owl, eagerly looked forward to lovemaking after the baby's late-night feeding. Claudia, the morning lark, barely survived feeding the baby, and all she wanted after that was sleep—blessed sleep. Missing each other's expectations just made us grumpy in the morning. Actually Claudia was more interested in sex at five in the morning, but Dave was asleep and the baby was crying. We both began to wonder if this were "natural" birth control?

Maybe you find yourself in a similar stressful situation. Your children are draining your energy, or maybe you don't have children but you're both working extremely hard in your careers. Time for loving is elusive and rare. Fortunately for us, in those stressful years, we could still talk about our love life, and both wanted to find a solution to our dilemma. Maybe some of our helpful discoveries will also help you. Yes, there was a solution and things did get better.

A Fulfilling Sexual Relationship Takes Work

Where do we get the idea that we enter marriage with built-in know-how? We learn to respond sexually, as we learn anything else, by working at it. We don't assume built-in knowledge in child rearing, our professions, or hanging wallpaper. Achieving success in any endeavor requires work, and sex is no exception. Even when things are hectic and crazy, you need to look for time to invest in your sexual relationship. Don't overlook the many excellent books that give suggestions for working on your love life. A fun one we suggest is *52 Ways to Have Fantastic Sex*[1] by Clifford and Joyce Penner. Another book we enjoyed reading was *Great Sexpectations* by Robert and Rosemary Barnes.[2]

A Fulfilling Sexual Relationship Takes Understanding

When we marry, we don't instantly understand each other. Before we were married, we felt we knew and understood just about everything about each other. But later we discovered that just wasn't true. Our friends Helen and George love each other and want to have a good sexual relationship, but they need help in understanding how they are different. Here is an example where they missed each other's expectations.

Helen decided to make this night special. Lately their sexual relationship had been bland, and she decided to spice it up. *First,* she thought, *I'll pick up George's favorite Chinese food, pull out the china and silver, and even use linen napkins and light the candles.* She splurged on a manicure. When George walked in the door, soft music played in the background. Helen was ready!

What about George? The main thing on his agenda was getting home to see the NBA final on television. At lunch George and his management team had talked about the basketball final. He knew that his team had a great chance to win it. His agenda was to get home, turn on the TV, pull up a TV tray, and watch his favorite team take the championship!

Helen and George had different expectations for the evening—and they were definitely conflicting. When George arrived home, Helen was ready for a passionate kiss and bear hug. Instead she got a quick peck as George headed straight for the TV. Talk about missed expectations. They were in conflict, but neither understood the other's hopes. The evening went downhill from there. George was so into the ball game that he missed Helen's cues. A drama was being played, and he didn't even know he was the villain.

Later as they were preparing to go to bed, Helen began to undress. George is a visual type of guy, and just seeing his wife undress aroused his interest. As he began to show a little loving initiative, Helen ran out of the bedroom in tears!

What was George's crime? He and Helen failed to understand their expectations and the different ways they responded to each other. George was stimulated by sight. If Helen had met him at the door in a raincoat (only), he might not have made it to the NBA final on TV. On the other hand, if George had given Helen the attention, tenderness, and romance she desired, her response would have been different too.

What about you? What puts you in a loving mood? What about your mate? Now there's something to talk about!

A Fulfilling Sexual Relationship Takes Time

Too often other things take precedence over the sexual relationship. You want to work on it but don't set aside time alone together. Remember, it takes time to communicate, to work through conflict, and to build a creative love life. Ten minutes after the ball game or TV news just won't do. Let us encourage you to make your love life a high priority. Your sex life can be a growing, exciting part of your marriage. It can happen even with little children. Here's how we did it.

We carved out a regular time each week when we could be alone without the children. One year we instigated "Monday Mornings." All three children were in kindergarten, or at Mom's Day Out. The house was ours. We discovered that there is nothing sacred about making love at night. Monday mornings were great! Your schedule may not be as flexible as ours, but find what works for you. For example, maybe you can hire a baby-sitter to take your kids to the park (or somewhere else if the weather is inclement) for a couple of hours Saturday mornings.

We started the tradition of going off alone together overnight. We began to realize that we needed extended times alone together—more than just a morning. So we looked for opportunities to get away. We couldn't afford to hire a sitter to come and stay with our children for an extended time, and our parents lived too far away. But we did have friends—very good friends—who offered to keep our three sons. We reciprocated by keeping their two girls, and we're sure we got the better deal!

Years later two of our early getaways stand out in our memories but for very different reasons. The first was a weekend we went to a cabin in Alabama. This was our first weekend to get away alone without our children, and it was "love city" from the time we got there to the time we left! Dave remembers the Alabama weekend as very fulfilling. Claudia remembers being oh-so exhausted.

The second getaway we remember is the week we spent at the beach in Florida. Claudia fondly remembers the slow pace of life, the long walks on the beach, romantic interludes, candlelit dinners for two, and shopping together and buying a new dress. Dave remembers it as a great week, too, but years later confided he was a little disappointed that we didn't make love every day we were there.

If we could live those years over again, we would talk more about our expectations and what is realistic for us. The key is to find balance and to come up with your own unique plan. While you're parenting toddlers, a fulfilling sexual relationship is not going to happen spontaneously!

You may want to talk about your unique situation and what you can do to make your marriage more of a love affair. Take a tip from us. To help you talk about your expectations, when you plan a getaway for two, discuss which of our getaways you identify with—the cabin in Alabama or the beach hotel in Florida. Where in your weekly schedule can you carve out some just-for-two loving time?

SEX IN THE LATE THIRTIES AND FORTIES

*L*et's jump ahead a few years, past the late-night feedings. Now our own teenage fantasies and sexual dreams become nightmares and fears for our own teenagers. An elusive and subtle fear may enter your bedroom. You may become more guarded around your adolescents. After all, you don't want them to get any ideas about how enjoyable sex is. Because of fear that your children will become sexually active, your own sex life may, without realizing it, become a lower priority.

Let us clarify. We don't advocate parading your sex life (or lack of it) in front of your kids. But you can pass on positive attitudes about sex to your children. Whenever the "S" word came up, we openly told our sons that sex in marriage is a wonderful gift. It's okay to let your kids know that skin on skin feels good. At the same time we stressed that they were not adults and encouraged them to reserve sex for marriage. We laughed when one of our sons filled out a high school form and put "not before marriage" in the blank that said *sex*.

We do know that attitudes are caught, not taught. It's not so much what you say as what you model. Do you openly give and receive physical affection? In *How to Really Love Your Child*,[3] Dr. Ross Campbell talks about the importance of filling your child's emotional tank with hugs and kisses. This is just as important for spouses—especially when you have teens! One of Dave's best childhood memories is seeing his parents out on the balcony, kissing and hugging each other. In the days of epidemic divorce, kids feel secure when they are assured—not just by words—that Mom and Dad really do love each other.

The adolescent years can add stress to any marriage. So we found some ways to combat that stress in our sexual relationship. Here are some things we learned during those years.

We needed to protect our own attitude toward sex. Even though sexual activity was not appropriate for our adolescents, we affirmed it was right, appropriate, and important to our marriage relationship.

We made a commitment not to let our teenagers crowd out time alone just for the two of us. Some of the ways we found time were by

- Using times when our adolescents were at school activities. You don't have to be at every practice game or choir rehearsal.
- Looking for alone time, like when our teens slept in late on Saturday morning.
- Soundproofing our bedroom. A stereo system or radio provides a noise buffer and adds to your privacy.
- Making sure our door was locked.

Don't let your teen's problems totally overwhelm you. Sometimes we can get too caught up in our children's situations. After all, this is a temporary stage. They do grow up and leave home. You want to nurture and enjoy your sexual relationship all of your married life, so don't let the stresses of life with adolescents short-circuit it.

Look for humor. Since teenagers and tension often go together, finding humor can help dispel it. Laughter actually helps us relax. During those years we tried not to take ourselves too seriously and to realize that much of what we were experiencing was temporary. And if we could find anything humorous, we laughed.

Do the unexpected! During these intense years, you can add the element of surprise by doing the unexpected. We've been known to do some zany things ourselves. Claudia will never forget the day Dave came in with three red roses and said, "Pack your bag. We're leaving in thirty minutes!" Remember, Dave is the romantic.

Off we went to a wonderful little hotel in the mountains about an hour from where we lived. Claudia wondered why they looked at her so curiously when we checked in. Dave had previously chosen the hotel and told them he had a very special lady friend he wanted to bring for a getaway. To this day, Claudia is convinced that the hotel staff didn't think we were married. Dave's reaction? "If you're going to have a romantic affair, have it with your spouse!" And that's just what we did. By the way, Dave included our three sons in on the planning of this surprise getaway for their mom.

What can you do that is a little zany? If you have teenagers, what are you doing to build a creative love life? Waiting for the children to grow up and leave home is not the solution. Or if your answer is, "It's just not that important to us," we'd like to challenge your thinking. Take it from us, this part of marriage can grow and become more enjoyable and fulfilling every year.

LOVE LIFE IN THE FIFTIES AND SIXTIES

One friend told us, "By the time we got to the empty nest, we forgot how to spell the 'S' word, much less say it!" We are in the empty nest. For years we looked forward to the extra freedom and flexibility we would have in our sex life when our last son left home.

Unfortunately, we developed a habit of work, work, and more work. Some of the time vacated by our son was swallowed up by book deadlines, marriage seminars, and parenting groups. While we could be more flexible and venture out, our lifestyle was too busy to take advantage of our new freedom. We simply tried to do more.

Again we needed to regroup. We tried to slow down and focus on each other. Old habits die hard. If you are a driven workaholic, your love life may suffer. Here are four ideas we found helpful.

Try new things. Move your lovemaking to new settings. Try out rooms in your house other than your bedroom and see what appeals to you. For instance:

- Maybe one of your kids who flew the nest left a waterbed behind.
- Consider that swing you just added to your secluded screened porch.
- Why not initiate the new carpet?
- What about an evening of nondemand touching under bubbles in a candlelit bubble bath?
- A game in which the loser must strip—one game you can both win.

All these suggestions are not from the Arps. We heard some of them at a follow-up group of one of our Marriage Alive seminars. The seminar had taken place eight months before, and this particular group had gotten together each month to share and encourage one another. That they had been successful was evidenced by this particular evening.

Each couple brought something that represented their marriage. One couple brought a green potted plant to suggest a growing marriage. Another couple brought a devotional book and shared how they were now praying together.

Amazingly, over half of the group shared something about adding creativity to their love life. From hotel receipts to whipped cream—this group was creative. But Joyce and Hank took the prize. They brought a tuxedo apron, a chef's hat, and a bottle of lotion. This empty nest couple told the following story.

One evening after work Hank volunteered to prepare dinner. Joyce, exhausted from her day at work, stretched out on their newly carpeted living-room floor and fell asleep. Imagine her surprise when Hank woke her up wearing only the tuxedo apron and chef's hat, with lotion in hand all ready to give her a body massage! Creativity was alive and well!

Another couple, who have elderly parents living with them, took a picnic basket and checked in at a local hotel for a couple of hours.

Eat healthy and get exercise. At this stage it's important to work at staying healthy and keeping physically fit. We used to play lots of tennis, but with our travel schedule, it's hard to schedule tennis on a regular basis. So we started walking together. We usually walk a couple of miles several times each week. And we're watching our diet. In the empty nest we're once again eating the vegetables we like, but our kids thought were yucky. By eating correctly and working on our physical fitness, we have more energy for the fun things in life.

Take the initiative! Be willing to take the initiative. Consider making arrangements for a weekend away, or plan a couple of hours each week when you can be completely alone. Maybe you could use a friend's empty condo or house for a date. You might want to try some of the following suggestions:

- Call and tell your spouse how much you desire him or her.
- Write a love letter.
- Give your mate an all-over body massage with scented lotion.
- Spend at least one hour talking and loving each other.
- Have your mate verbalize what pleases him or her.
- Give your mate an unexpected little gift for no reason at all.
- Buy a new mood music tape or CD.
- Tell your spouse ten reasons why you love him or her.
- Take an inventory of your bedroom. Make changes to create a more romantic atmosphere like adding candles, music, a light dimmer switch, a lock on the door. Remove all the books and paper work. Forget about your to-do list when you are behind closed doors.
- Make arrangements now to go away overnight.

SEX IN THE SEVENTIES AND EIGHTIES?

*R*ecently we visited an elderly couple, both in their eighties, both hard of hearing. It was hard to talk over the roar of the television. They didn't want to miss their soaps, and on this day the soaps were hot and steamy! From the hot tub, to the waterbed, to the beach, passion was acted out with fury. We began to realize that sex is still a focal point even in the senior years. But many elderly experience it only vicariously.

We hope we can be the exception, and, if we are, we'll write a book about it. In the meantime, we're going to keep working on our sexual relationship. To be honest, we are not to the soap opera stage. With all the "soap" passion and excitement, we wonder why those characters don't have heart attacks right and left! If sex is that great *all* the time, the Arps are missing out and probably you are too.

We conclude this chapter by confessing to you that our lovemaking is usually fine, sometimes fantastic, but always enjoyable. As the years go by, it keeps getting better, and we look forward to enjoying each other in our sixties, seventies, and eighties and as long as we are able.

What about you? It's your choice. Your sex life can be as fulfilling and exciting as you want to make it, but it takes time and work. But it's worth it. It can become better, more intimate, and more wonderful as the years go by.

Now is your opportunity to plan a great date! Maybe you will want to even kidnap your spouse. For other ideas, turn to Date Six in part 2.

Date Seven

Sharing Responsibility and Working Together

"If only we had more hours in our days, we could balance the two-job tightrope!" commented Louise. This particular Marriage Alive seminar was filled with frustrated two-career couples like Elliot and Louise.

Telling Louise that they had time—in fact, all the time in the world—didn't solve their dilemma. However, that particular session helped them come up with a workable plan. If you are among the many couples who both have jobs outside the home, we hope this chapter will help you find balance and devise a plan that works for you.

If you don't work outside the home, you may think this chapter doesn't relate to you. But if your four preschoolers—give or take a few kids—make an outside job look like a vacation, don't skip this chapter. You, too, can benefit by considering how you can work together to share responsibilities.

Stop to think of all the things we blame on time. How many times have you said, "If I just had more time . . ." or "I'll have more time when . . .

> . . . the children grow up."
> . . . the summer comes."
> . . . the summer is over."
> . . . I meet this deadline or finish this project."

May we suggest that time is not the real culprit? Time really is no respecter of persons. It's impartial. We don't have more time each day than you do. Everybody has twenty-four hours every day—no more and no less! The real issues are how you manage your time and how you work together. Let's take a closer look.

ASSESS YOUR RESPONSIBILITIES

*T*he first step in figuring out how to balance your responsibilities with your spouse is to assess your situation. You may want to consider your responsibilities outside of the home along with your responsibilities inside the home. If you arrange all your various responsibilities on a seesaw, putting yours on one end and your spouse's on the other, how would your seesaw balance?

For instance, if one mate is working outside the home only part-time and the other is working a sixty-hour week, the one who is home part-time would need to help balance the seesaw by carrying more of the load at home. But for now, let's assume you both have equal commitments outside the home. The important question becomes "How are you pulling together as a team at home?"

In spite of the many unrealistic stereotypes today—especially of the "macho males" who don't get their hands wet—we are delighted to see so many couples pulling together as they wrestle with jobs, children, and busy schedules.

Elliot and Louise, who are in their forties, grew up with stereotypes of men doing this and women doing that. The traditional roles worked well for them when their three kids were little and Louise was home as a full-time mom. But halfway through the parenting years, their circumstances changed. Elliot's company downsized. Elliot kept his job, but his bonuses were eliminated. Louise found a teaching job to help meet expenses and to save for their children's college expenses.

Elliot's daily routine didn't change. He worked as hard as ever at his job and came home just as tired. Louise's daily schedule changed drastically! Five days a week she came home tired, had lesson plans to prepare for the next day, and still faced the same responsibilities at home—the least of which was what they were going to have each night for dinner. Elliot was understanding and didn't say much about the frozen dinners, but not having clean socks and clean underwear irritated him. Tension built, and by the time Elliot and Louise came to our marriage seminar, they needed help!

A light went on when Elliot and Louise evaluated their respective responsibilities. Their list of responsibilities in the home looked something like this:

Louise's Responsibilities at Home

1. Prepare meals
2. Grocery shop
3. Do laundry for family of four
4. Keep the house clean
5. Keep track of children's activities
6. Arrange for sitters
7. Help children with homework

Elliot's Responsibilities at Home

1. Take care of the yard
2. Keep cars maintained
3. Keep family financial records

Elliot and Louise needed to make some adjustments. Elliot's home responsibilities were important and took time, but he could accomplish them on the weekends. Louise's areas of responsibility were not as flexible and daily demanded more than she could give after teaching school all day. They needed to redistribute the load at home.

Maybe you find yourself in a similar dilemma. If so, the first step is to list all household jobs and responsibilities and the requirements for each. Then look at the list and talk about who naturally enjoys doing the various jobs. Also, discuss those jobs you enjoy doing the least. Then go through the list again from the grid of who can do the job better.

When we did this exercise, we discovered that Claudia doesn't mind doing the laundry, so she took that on. Dave likes to grill, so he took over that responsibility. He also enjoys keeping track of our finances—a job that gives Claudia headaches! While talking through our list, Claudia immediately conceded that Dave was the best and most willing bathroom cleaner in ten states! But that was one job neither wanted to do!

The brutal reality is that no one will choose or want to do some jobs. Compromise is an important part of the process. Remember, you are trying to attack the extra pressures of having a two-job team, instead of attacking each other. You are also looking for understanding. We all can handle stress better if just one other person understands how we feel. You can be that other person for your spouse.

Once Elliot and Louise evaluated their situation, Elliot became aware of the stress Louise was experiencing and the need for his increased participation at home. The solution to his "no clean socks and underwear" dilemma might be to wash them himself. But the mechanics of who does what are not as important as the philosophy of attacking the problem together.

Elliot and Louise recruited their school-age children for jobs around the house. Louise was tired of teaching when she arrived home and loved being creative in the kitchen. She bought cookbooks for easy one-dish meals. With the Crock-Pot and a little planning she could have dinner on the way before she left for school. Elliot began to monitor homework and help with special school assignments.

For heavy jobs around the house, Elliot and Louse hired a cleaning service once a month. They found a high school boy who loved yard work and did the routine mowing and mulching. Elliot and Louise's seesaw may still go up and down, but on any given day it's much more balanced.

TILL DEBT DO US PART

One point of contention in many marriages is finances. Claire went to work to help with financial difficulty she and her husband, John, were experiencing. But Claire's working added tension. Listen to her story:

"When I went back to work, I thought I'd have some income of my own. But what actually happened is that my paycheck went into the same pot. John won't tell me where we are financially, and it's driving me crazy. I'd be better off if I just had my own bank account and helped with our general expenses."

Claire and John needed to work out their finances together. They needed to come up with a financial plan they both could agree on.

For us the real concern is not how many bank accounts you have (separate or joint) or even how much money you have, but that you have a realistic and workable financial plan that you both agree on. If you function best with separate accounts and it works for you, great.

Define Your Financial Goals

It helps to have well-defined financial goals—goals that you mutually agree on. We remember when we bought our first house. Claudia was a high school substitute teacher, and we saved her paychecks toward our house down payment.

In setting financial goals and working to achieve them, let us add one caution: It is possible to end up with all the things we would like to have, but no time to enjoy them. We can have it all and actually have nothing.

Delay Gratification

Dr. M. Scott Peck in *The Road Less Traveled* writes that a sign of maturity is the ability to delay gratification.[1] Yet we live in an instant world—instant oatmeal, instant coffee, and instant credit. Continually we hear that we can have it all and have it right now. If you are bored and have the right credit card, you can whisk your spouse off to a romantic island—no need to get baby-sitters (if you have children) or even pack. We are told to "Just do it!" Many problems in marriage could be lessened if we just learned to delay gratification!

The ability to delay gratification is part of emotional intelligence, so says Daniel Goleman in his book *Emotional Intelligence* (Bantam, 1995). He defines emotional intelligence as the ability "to motivate oneself and persist in the face of frustrations; to control impulse and delay gratification; to regulate one's moods; to empathize and to hope."

According to Goleman, emotional intelligence emerges already in early childhood. In one study, the "marshmallow test," four-year-olds were give a choice: either have one marshmallow immediately or wait twenty minutes, then get two marshmallows. The children who chose delayed gratification most often proved to be competent and successful teenagers. But the children who grabbed the first marshmallow frequently proved to be troubled and even delinquent as teens.

Coleman correlates the ability to delay gratification with successful living: strong marriages and families, responsible employees, and self-confident individuals. We suggest it is never too late to cultivate emotional intelligence and to learn to delay gratification.

Live with Less

And perhaps we need to learn to live with less. Living without something you've never had is not a sacrifice. Without the constant bombardment of advertisements and television commercials, we wouldn't even know about many things that we desire!

We make no claims of being financial advisors. We don't have it all together in finances, but we are working on it, so we can share some things that are helping us. One of the best and most practical books to use as a basic financial guide is Ron Blue's *Managing Your Money*.™² A helpful computer program is the financial planning software Quicken.

Other things we have tried follow:

- From time to time keep a record of each penny you spend. One or two months of this will help you evaluate where your money is going and to modify spending and saving patterns, which is not so easy, but possible.
- Limit credit card spending to what you can pay off each month. If things are really tight, we try not to use credit cards. Somehow, it's just easier to justify buying with a credit card. We sometimes say, "Well, I'll probably bring it back, and it'll be easier to return if I charge it." It may indeed be easier to buy, but a month later the bills arrive.
- Don't overlook the joy of giving. Several couples we know also have a special bank account. Each month they put money in that account, and from it they support their church and favorite charities.
- Get in the habit of saving. We used to say we just couldn't afford to save. The truth is we can't afford not to save. How much we save is not as critical as developing the habit of saving. Consider long-term goals—such as retirement and your children's education. Also consider short-term goals. If you have older children, you may want to choose a family goal. For instance, you might have a family garage sale to help finance an upcoming family vacation.

Choose Your Lifestyle Carefully

Only you can decide this highly personal issue. But you should make the decision together. Talk about your necessities. This will be different for each couple. Think back to when you were first married. Compare your living standards then and now.

What things are most important to you? How important are things like owning your own home, driving a new car, or having stereos, televisions, and video equipment? What about vacations, and meals out? Make your own list. Don't forget those less tangible things like time with each other, your children, friends, and your community and religious activities. List anything that requires an investment of time and/or money.

LIFE INVOLVES CHOICES

Collin and Jennifer were continually struggling to meet house payments and other obligations. Before the children were born, they both had full-time jobs and experienced little financial stress. Jennifer wanted to stay home with their two young boys, but economically it seemed impossible. After reexamining their priorities and financial goals, they realized that home ownership was great, but higher on their priority list was having more time to love and nurture their children.

What Collin and Jennifer did was brave. The sold their house and moved back into an apartment so Jennifer could stay home with their children. Tough choices await each of us. But at least we do have choices.

WHAT WILL YOU CHOOSE?

Some have more choices, but we all have choices to make. Louise went back to work to help provide for their family; Jennifer chose to stay home to nurture their preschoolers. No one can tell you what is best for you. But whatever your situation, look for ways to work together. If you both work outside the home, do it from a united front. You'll need all the communication and negotiating skills you can muster. Evaluating your expectations and redefining your goals will be an ongoing process. It was for the Whites.

Both Justin and Ann White's jobs required traveling, but neither was aware of how separate their lives had become. Then one day they met accidentally in the Los Angeles airport. Neither even knew the other was supposed to be in California! They were incredulous. Ann told us, "We looked at each other and realized that we didn't even know each other anymore. We had homes, cars, boats, but we didn't have an alive marriage. Standing on that concourse, we agreed something had to change!"

"That was a turning point," Justin continued. "We looked at our lives and knew it was time to make changes. We evaluated our lifestyle, and our list of necessities became shorter. We are both cutting back and slowing down. We have a long way to go, but we are making progress—and we are getting reacquainted with each other!"

Do you need to get reacquainted with your mate? We often hear, "We're doing it all for our kids—to give them more advantages in life." Noted child psychologist Dr. T. Barry Brazelton said that one key to successful parenting is to spend half as much money on your kids and twice as much time. Maybe that's also a key to an alive marriage—spend twice as much time as money. It's up to you. Look at your life. Look at your marriage. Chart your course. Both your marriage and your children will benefit.

Now it's time for another great date! Turn to Date Seven in the Dating Guide and get ready to have fun working together and sharing responsibilities.

Date Eight

Balancing Your Roles As Partner and Parent

"Enriching your marriage while parenting your kids sounds like an oxymoron to me!" Harriet, a young mother of three, continued. "I don't have enough time to be a good enough parent, much less a good enough wife!"

Both Harriet and her husband, Marvin, are committed to their children and to their marriage but have difficulty finding time for both. The result? Their marriage is usually the loser. While we felt her frustration, we didn't agree with her unspoken assumption: "Parenting responsibilities come before marital responsibilities." Do they? Should they? Does a parent have a choice? Obviously, urgent physical needs must be met first. But what about relational needs?

According to Dr. Paul Pearsall in his book *Super Marital Sex*, "As many marriages fail because of children as children fail because of faulty marriages. Until we learn that children are not special, but equal in importance to all of us, until we learn that we must not lead our lives and our marriages for children, but with them, we sacrifice our marriages, our own development."[1]

Marriage is the basis for family. It's simply foundational. Mom can love the child and Dad can love the child, but unless Mom and Dad love each other, the child can feel insecure. Did you realize that the number-one fear of children is that their parents will get divorced? So never feel guilty working on your marriage. When you are working on your marriage, you're also working on your family!

It's not easy to build your marriage while you parent your kids, but it is vital to the health of your marriage and your family! The good news is that it isn't an either/or situation. Your children don't have to compete with your marriage. The two relationships can actually enrich each other.

While in this chapter we won't share many parenting tips, we will share with you a new way of looking at your dual roles. First, we will consider how children can positively influence marriage, and second, how the marriage partnership can positively influence children.

HOW CHILDREN ENRICH YOUR MARRIAGE

*W*hat has the energy of an atomic bomb, provides more entertainment than a Broadway show, and weighs about seven and a half pounds? It's that first baby! The first child brings big changes for his or her parents. Do you remember when you transitioned from "just you and me against the world" to "It's you and me and baby makes three"? Nothing is ever the same again.

In the new world of parenting, however, words such as *tired*, *exhausted*, and *burned out* take on new meaning. We hear much about the strain that parenting places on the marriage relationship, but little about how having children can enrich a marriage. Just observing our grandkids and their parents remind us of ways our children caused our marriage to grow. You can experience the same. Check out these family-based marriage enrichers:

Children Remind Us That We're One

Little ones running around are a continual reminder that in a tangible way you are "one." Each time you see Junior's toes you have to admit they are just like Dad's, or that Susie's big smile is a picture of Mom's smile that won you over years ago and still melts your heart.

Think about each of your children. What traits did each child get from your spouse? From you? (Even if you have a blended family or if your children are adopted, you still pass on many of your traits and values to your children.) Look for them. Compliment your mate when you have the opportunity. "Robbie laughs just like you do—it's contagious and makes me laugh, too"; or "Jessie's got your great, big, blue eyes"; or "Annie has your pleasant, easygoing personality. What a wonderful asset in getting along with people!" Affirm your great observations. It will encourage your mate.

Children Foster Teamwork

Parenting definitely calls for a team approach. It's difficult for one parent to do it all. As young parents our evenings went better when we helped each other. We both looked for solutions—like when we hired our eleven-year-old neighbor to come over and play with the kids during the "suicide hour"—that hour in the late afternoon when Claudia was on her last leg and trying to get dinner on the table. Just giving your mate a coupon for one hour of "off-duty" solitude can build your marriage team.

Think of what you can do to team up with your partner. Brainstorm ways to lessen stressful situations such as "morning madness." One could assume the responsibility for breakfast while the other made sure the kids got up, got dressed, and stayed on schedule. At night when the kids are in bed, together you could talk about how to handle extra stresses you may be experiencing. Just knowing one other person understands your stress helps tremendously in handling it appropriately.

Children Promote Appreciation

Because the responsibilities of parenting leave less free time for two, you'll learn to appreciate each other in a new way. To be alone together is a real treat and one worth working for. When you have a couple of minutes, make a list of positive attributes that parenting brings out in your partner. For instance, "Hank's amazing patience with our children encourages me to not overreact when I get irritated with one of them." When you finally find those few minutes alone, share your list.

Children Promote Creativity

You will stretch your creativity if you try to spend time together when your children are small. You'll think of all kinds of ways to spend time alone. In one Marriage Alive seminar that was filled with young parents, we asked for suggestions for finding time together. Megan, the mother of six-month-old twins, reminded the group that even semi-alone time can be helpful. She suggested a stroller date. Your baby will enjoy the fresh air, and you'll enjoy the exercise and conversation.

Other suggestions from the group included the following:

- Plan a "Progressive Errand Date." Group your errands together. You can have time alone in the car as you visit the cleaners, post office, drugstore, and, on your way home, the frozen yogurt stand.

- Grab that time when your kids are at soccer practice. If you need to be close by, walk around the field together and talk.
- Go to a park that has a tennis court. Give your children plenty of balls and the two of you can sit down and talk. The tennis court becomes a gigantic playpen!
- Plan a getaway the same weekend as the band trip.
- If you have teenagers, plan on early Saturday morning to be your time together. You can count on your teens sleeping until noon!

Children Check Our Communication and Keep Us Honest

It's amazing what you say or don't say when little ears are listening. You're the model. It's enough to make us all stop and think before we speak. Just doing that would benefit any marriage.

We also learned we needed to be on the same track and say the same thing. Kids will ask you both the same question and then act upon the answer they like best. Our boys made mincemeat out of us if we were divided in our communication.

Use conversations with your children as a springboard to your own private conversations. Talk about how you are doing at saying what you mean and meaning what you say. Children are a reality check. If our talk doesn't match our walk, little eyes will see and report it. You may tell your children it's wrong to lie, but they hear you say, "Tell him I'm not home," when the phone rings and it's someone you don't want to talk to, or you look the other way when your twelve-year-old wants to go to a PG–13 movie. Children need parents who are honest and real and who admit it when they blow it.

Children Prevent Boredom

With children around, there is always something going on. You don't have to worry about sitting around in the evening and lamenting, "Oh, my, what can we do?" If you don't have plans, your kids will! Also children can help you relax and loosen up. Every family seems to have one joker who helps to keep things light and unpredictable. Your marriage will be more fun and less boring if you learn to laugh with your kids and at yourself.

Children Give Great Rewards

Witnessing our youngest son's college graduation commencement was a rewarding experience. As he and his classmates walked across the stage, a great sigh of relief from six hundred sets of college parents went up in unison.

It is rewarding to see our children launched into life. And part of that reward is all the memories of how your children enriched your life and marriage. You'll never run out of things to reminisce about. But we also send them off into life with numerous ways our marriage has enriched their lives!

HOW OUR MARRIAGE ENRICHES OUR CHILDREN

One of the greatest gifts we can give our children is parents who love each other. We've said it before, but it's worth repeating: The best way to help our children build successful marriages is to have one—an enriched marriage lived out before them day by day by day will fortify their marriages with all kinds of vitamins. Consider the following ways our marriage enriches our children's future lives and marriages.

We Provide Security, Love, and a Sense of Belonging

From Abraham Maslow's research on the hierarchy of human needs, the family provides those basic needs—home, shelter, safety, food, and clothing.[2] But it doesn't stop there. A healthy, enriched marriage provides children with a unique sense of security and love. As our children sense our love for each other, they are enveloped in that love. With this foundation, they develop a sense of belonging and identity. Marriage gives us a unique opportunity to influence the next generation and pass down a legacy of love.

We Model Healthy Relationships

Your children learn how to build healthy relationships by watching you and your spouse relate to each other in your marriage. Being able to relate to others in a positive way and build deep personal relationships is one of the great gifts we can give to our children.

What are you modeling to your children? Is most of the communication they hear relayed in the companionate pattern? From you they learn how to express their own feelings and deal with anger in a positive way. When our children were young, we taught them the feelings formula and would often remind them, "I hear some strong feelings and that's okay, but could you state that again and begin your sentence with 'I'?" Not only did it help our communication with our children, but it helped our children as they grew up, matured, and married.

We Give Guidance and Leadership

As parents, we are there to give guidance to our children. It is extremely confusing, however, if Mom and Dad are giving different advice. When we are united, we send positive messages. Our children learn to trust us. They know we aren't perfect, but they know we are real and that we are united. This keeps open the lines of communication and, even as adults, they feel free to ask our opinions. (And occasionally, we feel free to give them!)

We Teach Life Skills

The home is the first school for learning life skills. And since so many of those skills involve relationships, the marriage dyad is the ideal place to pass on life's most important lessons. You might want to make a list of lessons you learned from your parents. Then make a list of lessons you hope your children are learning from you. Things such as teamwork, stewardship, responsibility, boundaries, ecology—the list could go on and on.

We Pass On Traditions and Values

What an opportunity we have in our marriages to pass on traditions and values to our children and their spouses and families! While our children are not clones and will not reflect all of our traditions and values, their core beliefs often come from their home of origin. A good exercise would be, as a couple, to list your basic values and beliefs. What traditions are most precious to you? How do you model your core beliefs? Is it time to dig deeper and explore together the ultimate meaning of life? In the next chapter you will have the opportunity to do just that. In the meantime, enjoy counting the ways your marriage enriches your children and the ways your children enrich your marriage. Both you and your children are the benefactors!

Now it's time to have a date without your children. Turn to Date Eight in the Dating Guide and celebrate together how your children enrich your lives!

Date Nine

Developing Spiritual Intimacy

For the last eight dates we have focused on how to revitalize your relationship with fun, friendship, and intimacy. Now we want to focus on how spiritual intimacy can enhance the overall quality of a marriage. When we talk about spirituality, we are referring to your core beliefs and how they affect who you are and what you do. Your core beliefs influence all dimensions of your life and are played out daily in the values you choose and the choices you make.

For us, being spiritually intimate with each other is sharing the same core beliefs. It's having a shared purpose in life—a calling to something that is bigger than the two of us. It's our spiritual unity that sees us through life's storms and gives us inner peace in the midst of a turbulent world. We are convinced that having a spiritual dimension in marriage increases marital satisfaction.

Actually, numerous studies suggest that having a spiritual dimension in your life has a favorable impact on marriage. For instance, couples who frequently pray together are twice as likely as those who pray less often to describe their marriages as being highly romantic.[1] Also those who are religious are less likely to divorce, have higher levels of satisfaction, and higher levels of commitment.[2]

Some even go so far as to say that developing a shared belief system is central to having a healthy sexual relationship.[3] These findings make sense to us because having a shared belief system binds you together in the midst of dealing with problems and day-in and day-out living and loving.

Certainly marriage offers a unique opportunity for intimacy. It provides the time and opportunity for growing together spiritually. So in this chapter we will focus on how to develop spiritual intimacy through developing a shared core-belief system. Then we will look at how these core values impact a marriage relationship.

We realize that not everyone who experiences our *Ten Great Dates* will be religious or spiritually inclined. However, we believe that all have some core-belief system. Call it religion, a philosophy, personal ethic, whatever; your core beliefs shape who you are and how you relate to others.

What are your shared core beliefs? Perhaps this is an area you have never really discussed together. Are you willing to ask yourself hard questions and seek until you find answers? Then this date can benefit you. You can develop spiritual intimacy as well as couple intimacy. In the following pages we will take the liberty to share our personal search for spiritual intimacy in hopes that our experience might encourage your own search.

OUR SEARCH FOR SPIRITUAL INTIMACY

Our spiritual search began with a rather traumatic event. Married for almost four years, we were delighted that we were going to become parents. In the last weeks of the pregnancy, we discovered that our baby was in a breech position. The doctors, however, assured us that all was fine—until the actual birth.

"Please let this baby live!" Claudia begged while lying on the sterile table in the delivery room at Madigan General Military Hospital. It was 1966. We had spent the last three weeks moving into our army quarters at Fort Lewis, Washington, and getting the nursery ready for the birth of our first child.

Moving back to the United States after serving with the Army in Europe in the final weeks of Claudia's pregnancy was risky. But we had no other choice—Uncle Sam called and we answered. That day is etched in Claudia's memory:

"At the moment I delivered our first child, I didn't hear him scream, welcoming in the first breaths of life. I didn't hear the joyous cheers and congratulations of the attending physicians and nurses. Instead I heard medical professionals anxiously consulting with each other as they hovered over our child. I finally comprehended what they were saying: my baby wasn't breathing. Those tortured first few minutes seemed like hours. I knew by the faces of the doctors and nurses that what was going on was not normal, not something that could be fixed by a quick bottom slap. My newborn baby was in trouble.

"When I realized our firstborn son was fighting for his life, I instinctively turned to God for supernatural intervention on our child's behalf. And moments later David Jarrett Arp sucked in glorious, life-giving air, claiming this world as his own and us as his parents. My prayer had been answered!"

Though some might write this experience off as coincidence, we did not. Claudia was serious when she turned to God for help. And so strongly feeling a divine presence when her simple prayer was answered, we both knew this was the beginning of our spiritual quest.

OUR SPIRITUAL DISCOVERY

*B*efore Jarrett's birth, we had never paid much attention to our spiritual lives or our core beliefs. Until that fateful day in 1966, our lives had run pretty smoothly, and we didn't feel the need to examine our lives too deeply. Relating to each other was easy for us. We were secure in our love. Sure, we had the occasional disagreement, but we didn't experience any serious stress until our first son was born. Now we had just survived the trauma of an intercontinental move, a difficult birth with a life-challenging spiritual experience, and the incredibly common stresses of a colicky baby. Even though we were committed to each other and to spending some time making good on Claudia's delivery room commitment to find and understand God, we were suffering under the weight of life. Our marriage began to suffer.

For the first time we began to snap at each other and argue. It seemed that the harder we tried to make our marriage work, the worse things got. We weren't getting off to a good start as partners in parenting, and we didn't have the resources or skills to find any spiritual answers.

Fast-forward a couple of years. We had moved to Atlanta, Georgia, and were now expecting our second child. During this time we renewed friendships with friends from our college days and got involved in a local fellowship. We were raised in the Christian tradition and, finally, the spiritual seed planted in our childhood began to take root. As we asked hard questions about our own core-belief system, we slowly began to gain new insights. We began to understand spiritual truths that in the past had eluded us. And as we watched our energetic two-year-old, it wasn't difficult for us to believe there is a God who hears and answers prayers. Jarrett's antics—like demanding that we sit in the "night-night" chair until he went to sleep—kept us hopping!

During this time it helped that we were actively seeking spiritual answers. We began to read the Bible and our path to spiritual understanding was illuminated by God's love, acceptance, and forgiveness which, to this day, touch us to our very core. And as God began to be more real to us in our own personal lives, we began to experience spiritual intimacy in our marriage. It was as if we had been plugged into a new power source. Finding our security and significance in our Creator freed us to love and accept each other in a deeper way.

Our newfound faith gave us the courage to take risks and to be willing to grow. At the core of our belief system is a God who is involved in the daily lives of his people. Soon after we began our new spiritual journey, we had an opportunity to test it to the limits. While we loved being in Atlanta with our friends and near our family, Dave was not happy in his job. When a request to change divisions was turned down, he decided to step out and take a risk. (He didn't ask Claudia's opinion first!)

The day started no differently from any other day, but our lives would never quite be the same again. Dave called Claudia to say that he would be a couple of hours late, but he gave no explanation. Claudia assumed another big project had come up at work, never dreaming what was actually happening!

Claudia knew he had been frustrated in his job but wasn't prepared for his announcement when he walked through the door: "Honey, I quit!"

"But how are we going to live?" was Claudia's immediate response. We now had two sons. (Joel Hayden Arp had recently joined brother, Jarrett.) We also had house payments and a very tiny savings account.

"I'm really not sure," Dave responded. "But you know I've been dissatisfied at work. Well, I prayed about it. I prayed that the company would let me transfer to another division, but it didn't work out, so I assumed I was being led to another job somewhere else."

"Did you ever consider," Claudia said, "that you could keep your present job while you looked for another one?"

If you have ever gone through a job change (by choice or otherwise) you know that fear in the pit of your stomach that privately tells you, "I might starve to death." If our new core-belief system and faith in God could really make a difference, here was the acid test!

Dave remembers: "That was a hard time, especially for me, but in times like that our relationship needs a deeper dimension. Being spiritually transparent and intimate with each other helped. First, Claudia and I were able to pray about our situation. When either of us was afraid, we acknowledged that our spiritual bond would give us the strength we needed. Second, during this time I found my identity and significance as a person in the spiritual realm—in who I was and in my faith in God—not in job titles or in my accomplishments or lack of them. This gave me a real sense of peace in the midst of financial insecurity, and, of course, this affected Claudia as well. We believed and affirmed that our lives together had meaning and a purpose that was bigger than just the two of us. Finding our ultimate security in the spiritual realm enabled us to pull together and not push apart, so Claudia really tried to support me. We definitely had our moments, but the spiritual dimension is what got us through it.

"Several weeks later, the phone rang. An executive search firm representing a medical supply company was searching for someone with management and computer skills to open an office in the Atlanta area. Would Mr. Arp be interested in interviewing for this position? (I still don't know how he got my name.) I went through the interview process and within a couple of months was employed again.

"Though this story had a happy ending, this wasn't an easy time. I would not like to repeat it. But in thinking about this situation today, I now see how our spiritual unity allowed us to take risks, to step out of our comfort zone, and to grow closer to God and to each other."

Three decades later, our spiritual journey continues. We still have what we describe as a close, personal relationship with God, and this spirituality has impacted our lives in so many ways. Chief among them is in our marriage relationship.

Where are you on your spiritual journey? Can you relate to our experience? No matter where you are on your journey, we believe that every person has a fundamental belief system. If you focus on understanding your place in the universe, the meaning of your life, your relationships, and yes, your beliefs about the supernatural and God, your entire well-being will benefit. Plus, you can attain a greater oneness and loving connection with your spouse than you ever dreamed possible. But just what do we mean when we talk about this journey toward spiritual intimacy?

WHAT IS SPIRITUAL INTIMACY?

To us, the word *spiritual* suggests a realm and a higher being that are infinitely superior to human wisdom and impossible to fully understand. So anything in the spiritual realm requires faith that goes beyond human reasoning or understanding. The word *intimacy* means emotional closeness. When we use the two words together, spiritual intimacy means emotional closeness with our Creator, God. And our experience has been that emotional closeness with God contributes to emotional closeness with each other. This emotional closeness with God and with each other helped us through the time that Dave was without a job.

Drs. Les and Leslie Parrott shed light on the value of spiritual intimacy in a marriage when they write about "a shared commitment to spiritual discovery" in their book *Saving Your Marriage Before It Starts:* "The spiritual dimension of marriage is a practical source of food for marital growth and health. No single factor does more to cultivate oneness and a meaningful sense of purpose in marriage than a shared commitment to spiritual discovery. It is the ultimate hunger of our souls."[4] We know that, in our journey, our commitment to spiritual intimacy has helped to satisfy our hungry souls!

While spiritual intimacy defies a simple definition, to us, it has two main components that are easier to understand. First is the commitment to spiritual discovery and to defining your shared core beliefs. The second component is the function of how those core beliefs are lived out in your relationships.

Discovering Your Core Beliefs

Drs. Howard Markman, Scott Stanley, and Susan Blumberg, in their book, *Fighting for Your Marriage*, emphasize the importance of a shared core-belief system. They write: "A shared belief system—including mutual understanding about the meaning of life, death, and marriage—makes it easier to develop a relationship vision. In turn, having a relationship vision supports the long-term view of commitment."[5]

We have shared with you our spiritual journey and the basis of our core beliefs. Where are you in your journey? Have you identified your core beliefs? Do you have a shared vision? Is your commitment to your spouse long-term?

While the foundation of spiritual intimacy is a shared, core-belief system, we know that opposites attract and that partners do not have to agree on everything. But some fundamentals must govern the relationship. Some of our core beliefs include the following statements: Marriage is a lifetime commitment. There is a God who interacts with us and influences our lives. Prayer is an important part of our relationship. Respecting each other's individuality is essential to the growth of our relationship.

Other shared beliefs may include similar political beliefs, social and environmental concerns, and philosophy of parenting. Whatever the shared beliefs, they are the building blocks of an intimate relationship. They are the ties that partners cling to when outside pressures threaten the relationship.

You may be thinking that you don't have any shared beliefs—well you probably do; you just haven't taken the time to think about them or articulate them. Do that now. What are the fundamental values that you and your spouse share? What are the life principles that you both strive to apply in your marriage and family? On what aspects of your spiritual lives do you agree?

The Parrotts affirm the importance of searching for shared beliefs when they write, "Sharing life's ultimate meaning with another person is the spiritual call of soul mates, and every couple must answer that call or risk a stunted, underdeveloped marriage."[6]

We discovered that our common faith and beliefs gave us the opportunity to develop a deeper personal intimacy with each other. Thousands of years ago, King Solomon saw the value of spiritual intimacy when he said that two are better than one, because they have a good return for their work ... But even better, a cord of three strands is not quickly broken.[7]

Our relationship works best when we acknowledge that our marriage cord has three strands. What are those three strands? Dave is one strand. Claudia is another. The third strand is the spiritual dimension of our marriage. We see our marriage as a partnership with each other and with God. Many times we let each other down, and it's then that we look to the third strand to keep our cord strong, to hold us together when our individual strands are frayed.

Another story illustrates what we are talking about. In chapter 1 we told you about moving to Germany in 1973 and the strain this move put on our marriage when we moved on a very short six-week notice. But what we didn't tell you is how we even disagreed about moving in the first place! It was a crisis point. At the time we had three very small children and were happily settled in Knoxville, Tennessee. Move? Who would ever consider it? Dave did. Claudia didn't.

We spent many long hours discussing the pros and cons of such a drastic move. Dave saw the opportunities, adventure, and challenge of a new job. Claudia saw giving up her family, friends, and home that she loved and facing all the complications of moving and surviving in a foreign culture with three small, active boys. Dave was challenged. Claudia was scared. Time was running out.

We prayed together and we prayed separately about the possible move. Dave got peace. Claudia got panic! Finally, the deadline drew near. Were we about to give up the opportunity of a lifetime? There were no easy answers or solutions. We just couldn't agree! Claudia remembers:

"Without the basis of our lifelong commitment to each other and our shared purpose in life, I don't know what would have happened. I'll never forget the feeling of being totally out of sync with Dave; he felt so strongly about not passing up this opportunity. Finally I realized he felt more strongly about our going than I felt about our staying. Also I realized that his feelings were based on how our gifts meshed with the job opportunity, coupled with a strong conviction that God was actually calling us to Europe.

"My opinion was based on fear of the unknown and giving up what I did know. At that point, I made the decision for better or worse, for richer or for poorer, to go along with his strong leading.

"Was it easy? Absolutely not! It was the hardest thing I ever did. I was sure we had made the biggest mistake of our lives. Did I immediately feel at home in Germany? No way! I got there physically in July and my emotions arrived in February. But in the end, I was glad I took the risk. We went for three years, and we stayed almost ten years. We now call those years the golden years.

"But to be honest, if we had not been committed to each other and to God; if we had not felt there was a purpose in our lives and in our move to Europe that was larger than the two of us; and if we had not been committed to love, serve, and forgive each other, I don't think we would have made it. Our core-belief system held firm."

Perhaps at some time you faced similar crisis situations—an illness, a financial stress, or a broken relationship. Everyone has problems in at least one of these areas. Whatever fears and crises you are presently facing, now is the time to affirm those things that are truly important in life. You need to understand and affirm your core-belief system. It will help you develop spiritual intimacy and it will help you live it out in your marriage.

From a recent national survey we conducted on marriage, we discovered that a key to satisfaction and spiritual intimacy in long-term marriages is how the couple relates to each other—not their involvement in religious activities. Attending religious services did not guarantee spiritual intimacy. It is our daily choices based on our selected values that allow us to live out our spiritual intimacy. It is a function of our core beliefs.

Living Out Spiritual Intimacy

Have you heard the old admonition to love your neighbor as yourself?[8] This took on a fresh, new meaning when we applied it to our marriage. The key word, *neighbor,* means the person closest to you. And for any married person, the person closest to you is your partner, the one with whom you chose to share life at its deepest and most intimate level. If we love our marriage partner as we love ourselves, we will have his or her best interest at heart. We will want to serve, not be served, and we will resist the urge to manipulate or pull power plays. We will have a relationship based on love and trust.

So many times marital conflict would be resolved if we just loved the other as we love ourselves. Too often we are "me" centered and want things to work out "my" way. But just the opposite approach is what promotes spiritual intimacy. Consider the following ways we try to live out the essence of "spiritual intimacy" through unconditional love and acceptance, forgiveness, prayer, and service.

Unconditional Love and Acceptance

Central to our core-belief system is a commitment to accept and love each other unconditionally—not "I'll love you if ..." but "I'll love you in spite of . . ." However, this is not easy to do and many times we come up short! In "real time" it's not always easy to accept each other. Too often we react to surface issues—like the time Claudia got her hair cut too short. It was much shorter than Claudia had wanted and Dave's comment, "Makes you look older, doesn't it?" just made Claudia furious!

It's not always easy to accept that extra ten pounds you wish your mate would lose or to be kind when you discover your spouse mailed your income tax forms without signing them, or to have to economize because your partner blew a paycheck on a new computer printer you didn't need. And then we all have little irritating habits such as leaving used tissues lying around, or neglecting to return rented videos or library books, or not hanging up clothes before going to bed at night. Yet our basic commitment to accept each other helps us hang in there.

But in a spiritually intimate marriage not only do we strive to accept one another, we also strive to love one another unconditionally. Two thousand years ago, Paul gave some good advice to the people of Corinth who were having trouble loving each other unconditionally. He reminded them that love is patient and kind. When you really love someone, you don't envy him or her or get angry easily. Your love is to be forgiving, and you are not to keep track of wrongs or even notice the other's shortcomings.[9]

Does our love match up with Paul's description? Not always! It's hard to love like that. It's certainly not natural and, in our experience, it's the spiritual dimension of life that empowers us to live out this kind of love with each other. We have to continually realize that love is a choice we can make.

Sometimes we give each other unconditional love in the hard times—like when Dave's migraine headache just wouldn't go away, and we had to cancel our dinner out. Claudia chose to pamper Dave rather than complain. Or the time Claudia had a complicated root canal, and the dentist said, "Take a couple of aspirin when you get home and you'll be just fine." Whom was he kidding? Not Claudia! Through the throbbing pain that night Dave kept her supplied with ice packs and Jell-O™. At other times our unconditional love has been very conditional, but we keep trying.

Forgiveness

When we fall short in accepting and loving each other unconditionally, we rely on another of our core values: forgiveness. In Date Six we stressed the importance of forgiveness in a love relationship. Drs. Markem, Stanley, and Blumberg affirm the important of forgiveness for our mental health. They write:

> Forgiveness is a core theme for relational health. Long-term healthy relationships need an element of forgiveness. Otherwise, emotional debts can be allowed to build up in ways that destroy the potential for intimacy ... Marriages need forgiveness to stay healthy over the long term.[10]

We have found that being willing to forgive each other and ask for forgiveness helps to build spiritual intimacy in our relationship. As God forgives us, we can forgive each other. A forgiving spirit helps us to be more compassionate, tolerant, generous, and benevolent with each other. These traits help to build intimacy and trust in a marriage.

Prayer

Another core belief that affects our level of spiritual intimacy is our commitment to practice the discipline of prayer. Prayer is a unique spiritual resource in marriage. For us, praying together promotes spiritual closeness. In *To Understand Each Other*, the well-known Swiss psychiatrist Dr. Paul Tournier wrote:

> Happy are the couples who do recognize and understand that their happiness is a gift of God, who can kneel together to express their thanks not only for the love which he has put in their hearts, the children he has given them or all of life's joys, but also for the progress in their marriage which he brings about through that hard school of mutual understanding.[11]

Years ago we began the habit of praying together. Sometimes it's easy. Other times it's hard. When our relationship with each other is not running smoothly, it's difficult, if not impossible, for us to pray together. At those times we take a tip from our Quaker friends and try the Quaker practice of sharing silence. This allows us to worship according to our own personal needs, to seek communion with God separately and privately, yet be supported by the awareness that our spouse is also sharing in the experience. It's an easy first step in praying and worshiping together. According to the Quaker tradition, the devotional time is appropriately concluded with the kiss of peace.[12]

Service

We believe that our shared life must have a sacrificial quality, which leads to service. First we try to serve each other. Then we try to serve others. Marriages would be revolutionized if we had a servant's heart.

It's hard to learn to serve each other, especially in the closeness of a marriage relationship, but we quickly learned that it is an important part of developing spiritual intimacy. We never have functioned very well in our marriage when one or the other has to travel. It was especially hard when our children were small and Dave traveled a lot. He would come home exhausted and tired of people. One time stands out in our memory. He was selling data processing services and had worked for months designing a system for a company. This trip was to close the deal. At the last minute the president of the company reneged. All Dave's hard work was to no avail. He came home empty-handed. No signed contract! He was discouraged, ready to jump into his shell and hibernate.

What was Claudia doing during this time? She was home with a one-year-old and a three-year-old. Our older child had just shared his chicken pox with his baby brother. Claudia had been homebound and was itching to get out of the house and have some adult conversation. She was ready for reinforcements and couldn't wait for Dave to get home and help!

It didn't exactly work out that way. We were both so caught up in our own miseries that we didn't even think about serving the other. Claudia couldn't understand why Dave couldn't be more sensitive to her needs, and Dave just wanted to be by himself. We exchanged heated words accusing each other of being selfish.

After being miserable as long as we could stand it, we apologized and started over again. Years later we still get caught up in the web of "my" needs and "your" needs. We still have to apologize and start over. Knowing the principle doesn't mean that we always apply it. But it is our goal to do so.

Think of ways you can serve each other—like being sensitive to your mate's mood. If Claudia had not crowded Dave when he came home discouraged from that business trip, things could have gone differently. Or maybe you could give up what you want to do and defer to your spouse. Dave, before retreating, could have gone the extra mile and gone out with Claudia for a couple of hours or just offered to watch the chicken pox kids so she could have had a breather.

Second, we are committed to serving others. When we acknowledge that our life together is part of the divine purpose, we look for ways to live that out in service to others. We believe service promotes spiritually intimacy in a marriage relationship. Can you think of ways that together you can serve others? Maybe you are concerned about ecology and taking better care of our world. Or perhaps you would like to help Habitat for Humanity build houses for people who need a place to live. Your own place of worship offers many opportunities for service. For those who desire to serve, you don't have to look very far to find those who desperately need your help! Every time we get involved in serving others together, our own marriage seems to benefit.

NOW IT'S YOUR TURN

*I*t's very difficult to talk about developing spiritual intimacy without sharing one's own journey. We've taken the risk of sharing part of our journey with you in hopes it will motivate you to consider your own.

Let us encourage you to accept the challenge to develop a shared core-belief system. Be willing to open yourself up to your spouse and make yourself vulnerable. But please remember Dates Two and Three and the importance of handling each other's feelings with great care. Your marriage will be the benefactor. If together you are willing to seek answers for your own hard questions and define your shared core-belief system, you can develop spiritual intimacy!

Now turn to Date Nine in the Dating Guide and continue your journey toward spiritual intimacy together.

Date Ten

Having an Intentional Marriage

"I'm comfortable setting goals for our company," said Ralph, the executive vice president of a major corporation and a recent Marriage Alive participant. "But I never considered setting goals with my wife for our marriage. It makes sense. How have we survived twenty-five years without it? Is it too late?"

We were happy to tell Ralph and Norma that it wasn't too late. Whether you've been married ten years or thirty, it's not too late to set goals. It's not too late to have an intentional marriage—a marriage where both partners set goals and take proactive steps to improve and enjoy the relationship. It worked for Ralph and Norma, and it can work for you. You wouldn't be in chapter 10 of this book if you weren't serious about improving your marriage. Perhaps you have some great ideas and wonder how can you pull them together.

Sometimes it's not so much knowing what to do, but doing what we know. It takes three weeks to make a new habit and six weeks to feel good about it. In this chapter we want to help you work out your own action plan, and then, as you continue your Marriage Alive dates, you can have an intentional marriage, a high-priority marriage. We suggest a three-step process: First, review your past expectations; second, evaluate your present involvement style; and third, set your future goals.

WHAT WERE YOUR EXPECTATIONS?

The first step in having an intentional marriage is understanding the expectations you brought into your marriage. Some of your expectations were realistic; others were not. Sometimes at our Marriage Alive seminars we ask the participants what their expectations for the weekend are and why they came. Often we get unexpected answers: One couple came because babysitting was offered. Another couple came because they thought the weekend was tax deductible! But the Harrisons, a couple in their sixties, had another reason. They had paid the registration for their son and daughter-in-law. At the last minute the younger couple couldn't attend, and the Harrisons didn't want to lose their investment, so they came instead.

Mr. Harrison seemed very uncomfortable. When he and his wife discussed the first couple exercise, it was very quiet in their corner. As the seminar progressed, they relaxed, and by the end of the weekend, they were strong advocates of marriage enrichment. Since that seminar, we keep running into people who know the Harrisons, and we appreciate the free advertisement. They're recommending it to all their friends.

It's easier to adjust our expectations when, like the Harrisons, we start with few and are surprised at how great something is. But usually in marriage, it works the other way. We start marriage with stars in our eyes and a belief that our future mate is going to meet all our needs and expectations. Then when the honeymoon is over, our hormones settle down, and we get in the everyday rut, marriage may not be quite what we anticipated.

Plus, our expectations may be different. A group of teenagers were questioned about what they wanted in a mate when they married. One boy said he wanted an "old-fashioned" wife just like his mom, one who would find cleaning the house, cooking, washing, and ironing his clothes creative and exciting. A girl in the same group said she wanted to have an exciting career as well as five children, and she was sure that her husband would share home responsibilities fifty-fifty. We looked at each other and thought, if these two get together, they're going to need more than our book and seminar!

What were your expectations before marriage? Listen to what others have said:

- "The main reason I got married was for sex."
- "I expected my mate to meet my needs—to be a lot like me."
- "What I wanted in marriage was romance!"
- "I was looking for security and love, someone I could trust and lean on."

- "What was really important to me in my marriage was to have peace and harmony, to know that, when we went to bed at night, everything was okay."

Obviously, some of these people were shocked when their spouses were unable to live up to their expectations. Dr. Selma Miller, former president of the Association of Marriage and Family Counselors, states, "The most common cause of marriage problems is that partners' needs are in conflict, but they can't discuss the conflict because they don't know one exists. They only know they are miserable."[1]

It's important that we talk about our expectations. It's hard enough to meet expectations when we know what they are, but it is almost impossible when we don't know what our partner expects. Susie and Tom's marriage exploded after fifteen years. Unspoken expectations torpedoed their relationship. Tom wanted Susie to replace his best pal whom he'd lost in the Vietnam War. Susie wanted Tom to love and baby her as her dad used to do. They did not fulfill each other's expectations; they didn't even know what those expectations were.

What expectations did you bring into your marriage? Were most of them realistic? How have you dealt with the unmet ones? Are you still looking to your partner to meet them? Have you ever discussed your expectations? On Date Ten you'll have the opportunity to use our Expectation Survey to clear up any lingering misunderstandings and talk about your needs and expectations. (See the Dating Guide for Date Ten to preview the survey.) This survey will help you better understand each other's needs. Then you can intelligently evaluate your present marriage involvement style and together choose to modify that style to meet your deepest desires for your marriage.

WHAT IS YOUR MARRIAGE INVOLVEMENT STYLE?

*H*ow much intimacy and closeness do you desire for your marriage? Do you desire to share life deeply with one another? Most couples would say yes. To be loved, trusted, and appreciated, even when the other understands our weaknesses, gives us a sense of identity and self-confidence.

Where are you in your marriage today? Maybe you are not at the intimacy level you desire. The first step in moving closer is to understand where you are right now. Also, we need to understand that every marriage is unique. There are no right or wrong answers as to how much intimacy and closeness is ideal for each couple. This is up to you as you make your marriage an intentional one. To see where you are, consider the following chart.[2]

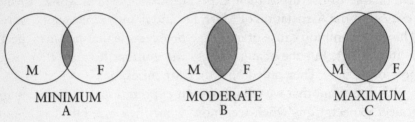

MINIMUM　　　　　MODERATE　　　　MAXIMUM
A　　　　　　　　B　　　　　　　　C

DEGREES OF INVOLVEMENT IN MARRIAGE

The three illustrations represent three degrees of involvement in marriage. When we talk about how our circles overlap, we're talking about both emotional involvement as well as time spent together. Let's consider each:

Minimum Involvement (A)

In a minimum involvement marriage, the lives of the husband and wife overlap very little. They have separate interests and hobbies and are usually quite independent of each other.

"I keep forgetting my husband is out of town," said an acquaintance of ours who has a minimum involvement marriage. We questioned the stability of their marriage, wondering why they did not experience more tension since they spent very little time together. For us, that distance would be uncomfortable, but it worked for them.

Maximum Involvement (C)

We have chosen a maximum involvement marriage style; our lives are deeply involved. We do seminars together; we write together; most of our friends and hobbies are the same. We make most decisions together and share our innermost thoughts and dreams. We even have desks that face each other!

Our circles overlap to a great extent, although we still have interests and activities that do not include the other. Actually we have to work on having a little separateness in our relationship. It's easy to have too much togetherness. Of course you can still have a maximum involvement relationship without working together. Perhaps you call each other on the phone five or six times a day to check in or consult on a decision, or your interests and friends are virtually identical—this also qualifies.

Moderate Involvement (B)

Most couples tend to fall in the moderate involvement range. Mike and Dianne work hard at keeping their circles overlapping at a moderate level. They are friends and lovers but also try to manage separate careers.

Mike is a talented young graphic artist and is definitely on his way up. When the opportunity to go into business for himself came along, he and Dianne spent many days and hours talking though the implications for their marriage and family. (They have two young children.) They decided to go for it.

Mike's hours are long, and he spends most weekends finishing urgent projects. Diane's job is not so stressful, though, and neither of them has a job that requires travel. Still, it's a real challenge to make their circles overlap at all. Rather than complain, they look for ways to work together to accomplish household projects. For instance, together they painted the outside of their house. They put up a fence in the backyard so that their kids could play safely, and they designed a rock garden.

For Mike and Dianne, it's hard work to stay in the moderate involvement zone. The maximum level is unrealistic for them, and the minimum level is below their expectations for their marriage.

How Involved Are You?

All three marriage styles are workable. In between these three styles is a wide range of varying shades and degrees of involvement. Where would you place your marriage? After going through these chapters, are you closer to each other? Do your circles overlap more or less? Do you agree on your own level of mutual involvement in your marriage?

Think back to the expectations you had when you said, "I do." If mutual activity was high on your list, do your activities reflect that involvement? If having a friend who goes through all the joys and sorrows of life with you was a high priority, does your relationship reflect that kind of friendship? If your answer is no, don't give up. Many couples have realized how different their marriage was from what they really desire and have been able to make a mid-course adjustment by answering the question, "Where would you desire your marriage relationship to be—in the A, B, or C circle of involvement?"

HOW INVOLVED DO YOU WANT TO BE?

The next step is to discuss together the degree of involvement you both desire. Compromise will be part of the process. Review chapters 2 and 3, especially the list of feelings words in chapter 2. Try to use the companionate pattern of communication and express how you feel without attacking the other or defending yourself. You may want to talk about things you would like to do together and things you would like to do separately.

The challenge is to find what works for you. Phil, a young doctor, told us, "When I get home, we immediately eat dinner—and that is usually late for the rest of my family. Then by the time we get the kids in bed and deliver the tenth glass of water, I have no energy left to work on our marriage. When Rita and I try to read a book on marriage (or anything), I fall asleep and that discourages her. Forget trying to do any written exercises or discussions. It just doesn't work for us at this stage of our lives. When we try to work on our marriage, we both get disappointed and give up. Where do we start?"

Our answer was to start with the time they did have. The most important question is "What are you doing with the time you have?" Phil and Rita had very little, but they did find some time. They now get up fifteen minutes earlier and start each day with a cup of tea and a quiet time together. They share their inner thoughts and feelings with each other and start the day in touch with each other.

Another medical couple asked them, "How in the world do you ever find time to do that every day?" They smiled and responded with conviction, "Oh, my goodness, we don't think of it as finding time. We have to take time. When we do this, we know we are centered."

Are you centered together? What is your focus? What are your expectations? Are they realistic? What is realistic in the early years of marriage before the kids arrive and after they leave the nest may not be realistic when you are in the trenches of family life with little ones or teenagers.

While conducting a Marriage Alive seminar, we stayed at a lovely bed-and-breakfast in the North Carolina mountains. The couple who owned the B&B were from Atlanta and had left the corporate world of sports cars and life in the fast lane. Visions of working together, plus the peace and serenity of the North Carolina mountains, had lured them to buy this particular bed-and-breakfast.

Yet we never saw them together! The wife shared, "Our circles don't overlap at all. Basically we work in shifts. As a matter of fact, our circles just keep getting larger and farther apart. We tend to go around problems, and we're missing each other completely."

It was time for them to regroup. Their expectations were unmet, partly because their expectations were unrealistic. Our advice was to try the fifteen-minutes-a-day time to touch base and regroup. Obviously they needed more time together than that, but at least it was a starting point.

After understanding your expectations and identifying your marriage involvement style, the next step is to set realistic goals for your marriage.

SETTING REALISTIC MARRIAGE GOALS

*W*hen we mentioned goal setting, did we hear you groan? Remember Ralph and Norma? Ralph wouldn't be where he was in his corporation without planning. Businesses thrive on goal setting, and marriages desperately need more of it! But few ever take the time to set specific objectives for their marriages, much less make a plan to accomplish them. Basically a marriage goal is a target toward which you agree to work. Here are the goals Ralph and Norma chose:

1. To improve our couple communication;
2. To become more creative in our sexual relationship;
3. To become more united and responsible in our finances, especially saving for our retirement;
4. To choose a common project to do together or choose something to learn together or do a service project for someone else.

Pick Your Major

Obviously Ralph and Norma can't work on all these goals at the same time. The next step for them was to choose a goal for the next few weeks. We encouraged them to start in an area in which they could quickly see some progress. Then as they were encouraged by their success, they could go on to more difficult areas.

Get Started

The next question is how to start. Three simple words guided them as they devised a plan of action: *What? How? When?*

What? What is the marriage goal you have chosen? Ralph and Norma chose to work on their couple communication.

How? Logically, the next thing they asked was, "How are we going to reach this goal?" The answer to this question needed to be achievable and measurable so they would know when they got there. How could Ralph and Norma open up their communication with one another? What activities would help them accomplish their goal? Here's what they wrote:

1. We will each read a book on communication and discuss it.
2. We will plan a weekend away in the next two months.
3. We will practice identifying our communication patterns and attempt to use companionate communication. We will not attack each other or defend ourselves!

When? Without answering this final question, Ralph and Norma would probably not reach their goal. This is the time they pulled out their calendars and planners and wrote in ink the time for doing the activities they had listed.

When you go through this process, if you are going to set aside Tuesday nights, then write the time on your calendar for every Tuesday night. When are you going to manage a weekend away? Pencil in several possibilities and begin working on freeing your schedule. What book on communication are you going to read? Block out time for reading. Then, like Ralph and Norma, commit yourselves to following your plan.

Perhaps like Ralph and Norma, one of your goals is to become more creative in your sex life. Again, you need to answer the three questions: What? How? and When?

What? Your chosen goal is "to become more creative in your sexual relationship." What can you do to deepen this part of your marriage that is measurable, achievable, and compatible with your other marriage goals?

How? Your short-term plans might be as follows:

1. Read *52 Ways to Have Fun, Fantastic Sex* by Clifford and Joyce Penner[3] and *Pure Pleasure* by Bill and Pam Farrell and Jim and Sally Conway.[4] Set aside two hours each week to be alone together for the next four weeks.
2. Plan a weekend getaway without the children in the next six weeks.
3. Make a list of creative things you both would like to do (give each other a back rub with warm scented oil, take a bubble bath for two, or play romantic music and light candles).

When? Next, make your schedule and commit the time.

1. We will read together Monday and Thursday before we go to bed.
2. We will arrange our schedules to be free for two hours for lunch on Friday.
3. We will plan a getaway for the first weekend of next month.
4. Together on Saturday we will make a list of ideas and put them in a jar to draw out at the appropriate time.

Monitor Your Progress

What about interruptions? You can be sure they will appear, so it's important to monitor your progress and be willing to flex when things don't go as planned. Some weeks your time together won't happen. Kids get sick, an unexpected project deadline must be met, drop-in guests appear, or other unforseeable things happen. But even if you don't follow through with every activity, you will be closer to reaching your goal than if you had not planned at all. So be realistic, but also persevere.

That's what Ralph and Norma did. During the last session of the seminar, Ralph and Norma decided that, besides working on their communication, they would also commit to having the ten dates in this book. Their goal was to have one date every week.

The first week, Ralph had to go out of town unexpectedly on business. He and Norma compromised and had a phone date. To add a little creativity and spice, they e-mailed love notes to each other. The second week, unexpected company dropped in. Once again their expectations were not fulfilled. The third week, another business trip came up. This time Norma's schedule was clear, so she went with Ralph and took their Marriage Alive date with them. They had their date on the airplane. It was so much fun they decided that, whenever they took a trip and flew, they would have an airplane date.

If your life is hectic like Ralph and Norma's, follow their example. Be creative and flexible. Whether you have your date on a plane, a train, in a doctor's waiting room, or in a coffee shop, spend time together.

Your final date awaits! Turn to Date Ten and get ready to develop a great plan for continuing your intentional marriage.

Postscript

*C*ongratulations! Completing your Ten Great Dates makes you Marriage Alive alumni. We hope your dates have given you a deeper love for and understanding of your spouse—that dating has helped you make your marriage a higher priority. We trust that now you can communicate on a more personal level and that anger and conflict are new friends—energizing your marriage and helping you to cope in a more positive way. You've become better friends and have a deeper appreciation for your marriage partnership. You've had the opportunity to infuse your relationship with intimacy and fun. But the challenge of having an intentional marriage is ongoing. So where do you go from here? Start by evaluating your ten dates.

HOW GREAT WERE YOUR TEN GREAT DATES?

*T*he following self-diagnostic test will reveal the progress you have made. To score, give yourself ten points for each yes answer.

_____ 1. I have enjoyed dating my mate. It's a habit I want to continue.

_____ 2. I log more time in the companionate pattern of communication. It's easier for me to share my feelings with my spouse.

_____ 3. My spouse and I signed the contract not to attack each other or defend ourselves and are abiding by it—most of the time.

_____ 4. I gave my spouse a compliment sometime in the last twenty-four hours.

_____ 5. I am satisfied with our current marriage involvement style.

_____ 6. I have gained new insights about my spouse that I didn't know or understand previously.

_____ 7. My spouse and I have made concrete plans for a romantic getaway.

_____ 8. I have taken out the garbage (cleaned the toilets, or whatever it is you really don't like to do) in the past seven days.

_____ 9. I am willing to give up something I want to do in order to do something my spouse wants to do.

_____ 10. I have a new excitement and enthusiasm about my marriage and just can't wait until our next date!

Add up your score and rate yourself on the following scale:

100	Fantastic! You're a ten! You qualify as a Marriage Alive Ten Great Dates guide. Find another couple (or two or three!) to personally escort through their ten dates.
80–90	Great! You're in the process of building an alive, enriched marriage. Keep up the good work and stick to your plan.
60–70	Not bad. Don't give up. Acknowledge your successes and choose another area to work on.
50 or below	Turn back to page one. Repetition is a great teacher.

Whatever your score, by completing these ten great dates you have shown you have what it takes to have an alive, growing marriage. Now comes the responsibility to continue in the things you have learned and to pass them on to other couples.

YOUR MARRIAGE CAN BE A LIGHTHOUSE!

Many marriages today are functioning way below their potential. But you can do something about it—your marriage can light the way for others. We need a widespread movement of couples choosing to prioritize their marriage, to date their mate, and to encourage other couples to do the same. Over the years, couples like our dear friends and mentors, David and Vera Mace, have modeled how to have a positive and growing marriage. They willingly became involved in our lives by loving, encouraging, and supporting our desire to have an alive marriage. And with the strong foundation that the Maces and other couples built as they developed the marriage enrichment movement, we now are able to help other couples experience what has been passed on to us.

One of the great benefits of our work in marriage enrichment over the years is that it has motivated us to continue to work at having our own intentional marriage. As you have probably gleaned from the pages of this book, our marriage is still in process. While compiling the many dating exercises for this book and leading our Marriage Alive seminars, we continue to work on our own marriage relationship. Please do not consider your Ten Great Dates a one-time experience. We know couples who repeat these ten dates each year as a marriage check-up.

As we continue to work on our own marriage, we can encourage others to do the same. Wouldn't you like to join with us? Your marriage can be a lighthouse. Are you willing to take the torch and pass on to others the message of how to have an enriched, healthy marriage? Then start your own dating club.

START YOUR OWN MARRIAGE ALIVE DATING CLUB

If you start a fire with only one log, the flame may go dim, but several logs together burn brightly. To keep the fires of your marriage burning brightly, consider starting your own Marriage Alive Dating Club. You could organize a Couple's Nights Out™ group or simply invite a few other couples into your home. Commit yourselves to each other to be that encourager to keep on building a truly enriched, alive marriage.

You could use this book as your guide. One format that has worked well for many groups is to get together monthly. Discuss one date each month and commit to have the corresponding date between your times together. It really helps to have supportive friends who gently nudge you to grow your marriage.

CELEBRATE YOUR MARRIAGE!

Fun and celebration are like vitamins for the soul. And they are good for your marriage's health. An enriched, fun-loving marriage can make a difference in your quality of life. So as you continue dating take time to celebrate that your marriage is truly alive!

Notes

DATE TWO—Learning to Talk

1. Alan Loy McGinniss, *The Friendship Factor: How to Get Closer to the People You Care For* (Minneapolis: Augsburg, 1979), 103–4

2. We are grateful to David and Vera Mace for their input into our lives and marriage and for the excellent training we received from the Association of Couples in Marriage Enrichment (A.C.M.E.) Training Workshops with David and Vera Mace. Our basic philosophy of the three patterns of communication and how to deal with anger and conflict is adapted from our training with the Maces and used with their permission. A.C.M.E. offers excellent leadership training for those interested in leading marriage enrichment groups. For more information about A.C.M.E. or their training workshops, write to A.C.M.E., P.O. Box 10596, Winston-Salem, NC 27108, or call 1-800-634-8325.

3. We first learned the concept of the feelings formula from Bill and Kathy Clarke who for years have conducted Marriage and Family Enrichment Institutes. We met the Clarkes when we were just beginning our work in marriage enrichment and their input over the years has enriched our own work in marriage and family enrichment.

4. Norman Wright, *Communication and Conflict Resolution in Marriage* (Elgin, IL: David C. Cook, 1977), 6.

DATE THREE—Resolving Honest Conflict

1. David Mace, *Close Companions* (New York: Continuum, 1982), 85.

2. We thank Doug Wilson for sharing his illustration of animal characters with us in Vienna, Austria, in 1981 and giving us permission to adapt his concept for use in our work in marriage enrichment. Doug and his wife, Karen, spent several days with us when we were first designing our Marriage Alive seminar and gave strategic input that has benefited us and many other couples through the years.

3. Howard Markman, Scott Stanley, and Susan L. Blumberg, *Fighting for Your Marriage* (San Francisco: Jossey-Bass Publishers, 1994), 76. Drs. Markman, Stanley, and Blumberg are marital researchers and founders of PREP™ (The Prevention and Relationship Enhancement Program). PREP™

is a research-based approach to teaching couples how to communicate effectively, work as a team to solve problems, manage conflicts without damaging closeness, and preserve and enhance commitment and friendship. The PREP approach is based on twenty years of research in the field of marital health and success, with much of the specific research conducted at the University of Denver over the past fifteen years. For more information about PREP write to PREP, Inc., P. O. Box 102530, Denver, CO 80250 or call 1–303–759–9931.

4. Adapted from David and Vera Mace, *How to Have a Happy Marriage* (Nashville: Thomas Nelson, 1992).

5. Our four steps for resolving conflict were originally adapted from H. Norman Wright's book, *The Pillars of Marriage* (Glendale, CA: Regal, 1979), 158. This is just one of Norm Wright's many excellent marriage enrichment resources. We wish to express our deep appreciation to Norm for his influence in not only our lives and work but in many others' lives as well.

6. Adapted from David Mace, *Love and Anger in Marriage* (Grand Rapids: Zondervan, 1982), 109–12.

7. Dr. John Gottman, *Why Marriages Succeed or Fail* (New York: Simon & Schuster, 1994), 29.

8. Ibid.

DATE FOUR—Becoming an Encourager

1. Dr. John Gottman, *Why Marriages Succeed or Fail* (New York: Simon & Schuster, 1994), 29.

DATE FIVE—Finding Unity in Diversity

1. The Myers-Briggs Type Indicator is available through Consulting Psychologist Press, Inc., 557 College Avenue, Palo Alto, CA 94306. The Taylor-Johnson Temperament Analysis is available from Psychology Publications, 5300 Hollywood Blvd., Los Angeles, CA 90027. Marital Evaluation Checklist ™ is available from Psychological Assessment Resources, Inc., P.O. Box 998, Odessa, FL 33556.

DATE SIX—Building a Creative Love Life

1. Clifford Penner, *52 Ways to Have Fun, Fantastic Sex* (Nashville: Thomas Nelson, 1994).

2. Robert and Rosemary Barnes, *Great Sexpectations* (Grand Rapids: Zondervan, 1996).

3. Dr. Ross Campbell, *How to Really Love Your Child*, (Wheaton, IL: Victor Books, 1978).

DATE SEVEN—Sharing Responsibility and Working Together

1. M. Scott Peck, *The Road Less Traveled* (New York: Walker, 1985).

2. Ron Blue, *Managing Your Money*™ (Nashville: Thomas Nelson, 1993)

DATE EIGHT—Balancing Your Dual Role As Partner and Parent

1. Paul Pearsall, *Super Marital Sex* (New York: Ballantine, 1987), 16.

2. Abraham Maslow, *Motivation and Personality* (New York: Worth, 1970).

DATE NINE—Developing Spiritual Intimacy

1. Les and Leslie Parrott, *Saving Your Marriage Before It Starts* (Grand Rapids: Zondervan, 1995), 145.

2. Howard Markman, Scott Stanley, and Susan L. Blumberg, *Fighting for Your Marriage* (San Francisco: Jossey-Bass, 1994), 285.

3. Paul Pearsall, *Super Marital Sex* (New York: Ballantine, 1987), 217.

4. Les and Leslie Parrott, *Saving Your Marriage Before It Starts* (Grand Rapids: Zondervan, 1995), 135.

5. Markman, Stanley, and Blumberg, 292.

6. Parrott, 135.

7. Ecclesiastes 4:9–12.

8. Matthew 19:19.

9. 1 Corinthians 13:4–5.

10. Markman, Stanley, and Blumberg, 294.

11. Paul Tournier, *To Understand Each Other* (Atlanta: John Knox, 1967), 60.

12. David and Vera Mace, *What's Happening to Clergy Marriages?* (Nashville: Abingdon, 1980), 103–4.

DATE TEN—Having an Intentional Marriage

1. Mary Susan Miller, "What Are Your Expectations from Marriage?" *Family Life Today* (October 1980), 76.

2. David and Vera Mace, *We Can Have Better Marriages if We Really Want Them* (Nashville: Abingdon, 1974), 76.

3. Clifford and Joyce Penner, *52 Ways to Have Fun, Fantastic Sex* (Nashville: Thomas Nelson, 1994).

4. Bill and Pam Farrell; Jim and Sally Conway, *Pure Pleasure* (Downers Grove: InterVarsity, 1994).

Ten Great Dates to Energize Your Marriage
Video Curriculum

A video-based resource for enriching marriages
and for starting Couples' Nights Out™

Get Ready for FUN!

Drawing on the best tips from David and Claudia Arp's popular Marriage Alive Seminars, *Ten Great Dates to Energize Your Marriage* video resource helps spark romance with memory-making evenings built on key, marriage-enriching themes. Enjoy your dates alone as a couple, or use this resource to initiate an ongoing marriage enrichment program.

By providing free or low-cost child care and fun, short, video date launches, you can start Couples' Nights Out. You'll help connect couples with other couples during the date launch and also provide time alone for each couple to explore the topic discussed earlier. A marriage enrichment strategy that works for groups of all sizes and in all stages of marriage, its benefits include:

- Dates with a purpose
- Involvement of both spouses
- Time alone for each couple
- Low-key topical discussion starters
- Easy start-up
- FUN!

Ten Great Dates to Energize Your Marriage contains:

- two 75-minute videos with ten short date launches
- one *Ten Great Dates to Energize Your Marriage* (softcover, 208 pages)
- one Leader's Guide (48 pages)

Extra books for each couple are available separately. Included in the book is a dating guide and duplicate tear-out exercises for each date. May be ordered through your local bookstore.

ISBN 0-310-21350-9
Video Curriculum Kit

Second Half of Marriage

Facing the Eight Challenges of Every Long-Term Marriage

"The Arps have blazed a trail to the real 'better half' of marriage."

Gold Medallion Winner

David and Claudia Arp discovered the enormous potential of marriage's second half after dropping off their last child at college. Suddenly, after thirty years of marriage, the Arps were "empty nesters"—and they had one important question: "How can we make the second half of our marriage better than the first?"

Their search for an answer led them to survey hundreds of couples facing the same life circumstances. What they learned, coupled with their own seasoned insights, can make the difference in your marriage as well. *The Second Half of Marriage* will challenge you to create a vision for the rest of your life together—and inspire you to make that vision a reality. This unique book shows you:

- Eight marital challenges that every long-term couple faces
- Practical strategies to meet each challenge
- Fascinating findings from the Arps' national marriage survey
- Insightful comments from second-half couples
- The revealing story of a couple who has creatively mastered the challenges of marriage's second half
- Exercises to help you apply the principles of this book to your marriage

"The Arps have blazed the trail to the real 'better half' of marriage—and the best is yet to come. Your first step is to get this book. Your second is to take a hike—together!"

— Scott Stanley, Ph.D.
Center for Marital Studies, University of Denver,
co-author of *Fighting for Your Marriage*

Hardcover
ISBN 0-310-20714-2
Audio pages 0-310-20978-1

Seminars
with David and Claudia Arp

THE MARRIAGE ALIVE SEMINAR

An exciting, fun-filled approach to building thriving marriages. Topics covered are prioritizing your marriage, finding unity in diversity, communicating your feelings, processing anger and resolving conflict, and cultivating spiritual intimacy. Use this 6-hour seminar to jump-start your own Couples' Nights Out™ group!

> *"Through the personal sharing of their own marital experience, Dave and Claudia make available a wealth of ideas, practical suggestions, and inspiration for couples who care about their marriage and want to make it stronger, deeper, and more fulfilling."*
>
> —Dr. Vera Mace, author and co-founder of the American Association of Marriage and Family Therapy (A.A.M.F.T.) and the Association for Couples in Marriage Enrichment (A.C.M.E.)

THE PARENTING SEMINAR

Designed to help develop positive family dynamics, add fun and focus to family life, and build supportive relationships with other parents, this seminar's focus can be general or specifically targeted to parents to help them get ready for and survive the adolescent years.

> *"MOM's & DAD's Support Group video-based parenting program is a must for all parents—especially those parenting alone. The Arps are an outstanding resource in the field of marriage and family enrichment. I strongly recommend them to anyone looking for resources."*
>
> —Larry L. Eakes, Chaplain (MAJ), U.S. Army

THE SECOND HALF OF MARRIAGE SEMINAR

The Arps reveal eight challenges that all long-term marriages face and give practical strategies to meet each. Topics covered include choosing a partner-focused marriage, renewing the couple friendship, focusing on the future, and growing together spiritually. A timely seminar as baby boomers turn 50!

About the Authors

Claudia Arp and David Arp, MSSW, a husband-wife team, are founders of Marriage Alive International, a ground-breaking ministry dedicated to providing resources and training to empower congregations to help build better marriages and families. Their Marriage Alive seminar is popular across the U.S. and in Europe.

The Arps are well-known conference speakers, columnists, and authors of numerous books and video curricula including *10 Great Dates* and the Gold Medallion Award-winning *The Second Half of Marriage.* Frequent contributors to print and broadcast media, Dave and Claudia have appeared as empty nest experts on the NBC *Today Show*, CBS *This Morning* and Focus on the Family. Their radio program, *The Family Workshop,* is heard daily on over 200 stations. David and Claudia have been married for over 35 years and have 3 married sons and 7 grandchildren. Visit their website at www.marriagealive.org

To schedule the Arps for a Marriage Alive seminar or other speaking engagements or for information about other Marriage Alive resources contact:

Marriage Alive International
51 West Ranch Trail
Denver, CO 80465
Phone: (888) 690-6667
Email: mace@marriagealive.org
Website: www.marriagealive.com

Marriage Alive
COUPLE ENRICHMENT
RESOURCE

Part Two

The Marriage Alive
Dating Guide

Welcome to Your
Marriage Alive Ten Great Dates

Welcome to your personal Marriage Alive Ten Great Dates! We're glad you're taking the time to grow together by dating your mate. We hope you will relax and enjoy focusing on your marriage relationship. You'll have the opportunity to see your marriage more clearly, get to know yourself and your mate better, pay attention to each other, and laugh and affirm one another.

Each date has been crafted to help you concentrate on a specific marital skill. We've taken care of the details so you can concentrate on each other. You'll find pre-date suggestions for how to prepare for your date with ideas for where to go, how to approach each date, and how to benefit from the exercises.

While it's desirable for each partner to read the corresponding chapter before the date and fill out the exercise, we realize sometimes this just won't happen. So with each date we have included a brief chapter summary.

These dates are based on more than two decades of experience and practical input from couples who have participated in Marriage Alive seminars and dates. You can trust each date to be a faithful guide in enriching your relationship. So come escape from the daily cares and routine. Get ready for a "growth leap" in your marriage!

We trust that this investment of time will reap great dividends as you grow together in your marriage relationship!

Blessings,
David & Claudia

Your Marriage Alive Dating Plan

Write in when you are going to have each date.

Date One, Choosing a High-Priority Marriage,
    is scheduled for _____

Date Two, Learning to Talk,
    is scheduled for _____

Date Three, Resolving Honest Conflict,
    is scheduled for _____

Date Four, Becoming an Encourager,
    is scheduled for _____

Date Five, Finding Unity in Diversity,
    is scheduled for _____

Date Six, Building a Creative Love Life,
    is scheduled for _____

Date Seven, Sharing Responsibility and Working Together,
    is scheduled for _____

Date Eight, Balancing Your Dual Role As Partner and Parent,
    is scheduled for _____

Date Nine, Developing Spiritual Intimacy,
    is scheduled for _____

Date Ten, Having an Intentional Marriage,
    is scheduled for _____

Your Dating Ground Rules

Before you date, please read this.

To get the most out of each date we make the following suggestions:

- *Read the corresponding chapter and/or the chapter summary.* If you have not filled out the exercise, do so before you begin your discussion.
- *Stay positive!* All of us have things we'd like to tell our spouse. This is NOT the time to tell your mate what he or she has done wrong the past ten years.
- *Be future focused.* Focus on what you want your relationship to be like in the future. Don't concentrate on past failure. (It's okay to remember past successes.)
- *Talk about your relationship.* Do not talk about your children, job, mother-in-law, or other things outside your relationship.
- *Give a gift of love.* Some dates will interest you more than others. On the less exciting ones, give a gift of love: Participate enthusiastically!
- *Don't force it.* If you have difficulty on a particular date or get on a negative track, stop that discussion. Move on to another topic that you both feel good about. Do something that is fun, like bowling, tennis, taking a walk, or eating cake.
- *Use good communication skills.* Be prepared for some surprises and new insights about your spouse. They can open new opportunities for growth and intimacy in your marriage. Following are several tips for sharing your answers:

  1. Be honest, yet never unkind.
  2. Remember to start your sentences with "I" and let them reflect back on you.
  3. Resist attacking the other or defending yourself.
  4. Use the feelings formula when you are able.
  5. Be specific and positive.

- *Have fun!* Remember why you are dating your mate. It is to enrich and put new life into your marriage. It's simply imperative to have fun along the way!
- *After each date, take the post-date application tips seriously!* Remember, you are developing healthy habits that will enrich your marriage long after your Marriage Alive Ten Great Dates have been completed.

Date One

Choosing a High-Priority Marriage

PRE-DATE PREPARATION

- Read Chapter 1, "Choosing a High-Priority Marriage." Fill out Date One Exercise. Filling out the exercises before your date gives time for reflection. Also if one of you is more verbal than the other, writing will give you time to formulate your thoughts.
- Make reservations at a favorite restaurant. (The one making the reservations may want to let the place be a surprise.)
- If applicable, make arrangements for the children. Get a baby-sitter if needed. This could be set up on a regular weekly basis for ten weeks.
- Think about what you will wear. Choose an outfit you think your spouse would like. Remember, this is a date!

DATE NIGHT TIPS

- Plan to use the whole evening. (Don't think about rushing home for your favorite TV program. If there is something you have to see, use your VCR and record it for another evening.)
- During a leisurely dinner take your own trip down memory lane. You can use the Memory Lane Exercise (part 1) to jog your memory. Talk about your history.
- Part 2 of the date exercise will help you focus on the present and what is positive about your marriage at this stage of life. Allow enough time for each question and take turns in sharing your answers.
- Before you start, review communication tips in the Dating Ground Rules, page 148.

CHAPTER SUMMARY

From our own time of crisis in the early seventies, we chose three goals to help us make our marriage a priority. By reviewing these goals from time to time, we have built a high-priority marriage, and you can too. The first goal is to look at and evaluate where your marriage is right now. The second goal is to set goals for the future. The third goal is to learn new relational skills to help your marriage grow. On this date, you'll have the opportunity to review your past and look at your marriage as it is today. We suggest also reviewing the three principles for building a successful, high-priority marriage: Put your marriage first; commit to grow together; and work at staying close. You can make your marriage a high priority!

DATE ONE EXERCISE

PART 1—A Trip Down Memory Lane

First time I saw my mate: _____
_____
_____

First date: _____
_____
_____

First kiss: _____
_____
_____

Favorite dates: _____
_____
_____

First time we talked about getting married: _____
_____
_____

Wedding day: _____
_____
_____

First home: _____
_____
_____

First anniversary: _____
_____
_____

Most romantic moments: _____
_____
_____

Happiest memories: _____
_____
_____

PART 2—What's Great About Us!

1. What are three things that are positive about our marriage relationship?

    1. _____
    2. _____
    3. _____

2. What are two things that are fine about our relationship but could be better?

    1. _____
    2. _____

3. What is one thing I personally could do to make our relationship better?

    1. _____

POST-DATE APPLICATION

- Look for ways to compliment each other between now and the next date. Give at least one honest compliment each day.
- Do one thing to make your marriage better.

DATE ONE EXERCISE

PART 1—A Trip Down Memory Lane

First time I saw my mate: _____
_____
_____

First date: _____
_____
_____

First kiss: _____
_____
_____

Favorite dates: _____
_____
_____

First time we talked about getting married: _____
_____
_____

Wedding day: _____
_____
_____

First home: _____
_____
_____

First anniversary: _____
_____
_____

Most romantic moments: _____
_____
_____

Happiest memories: _____
_____
_____

PART 2—What's Great About Us!

1. What are three things that are positive about our marriage relationship?

   1. _____

   2. _____

   3. _____

2. What are two things that are fine about our relationship but could be better?

   1. _____

   2. _____

3. What is one thing I personally could do to make our relationship better?

   1. _____

POST-DATE APPLICATION

- Look for ways to compliment each other between now and the next date. Give at least one honest compliment each day.
- Do one thing to make your marriage better.

Date Two

Learning to Talk

PRE-DATE PREPARATION

- Read Chapter 2, "Learning to Talk." Reflect on Date Two Exercise.
- Choose a location that will allow you to talk quietly—perhaps a picnic in a park or a quiet coffee shop.

DATE NIGHT TIPS

- Discuss your exercise, point by point. Alternate who goes first, just like you did on Date One.
- Be prepared for some surprises and new insights about your spouse. This new knowledge can add depth to your relationship.
- Review communication tips in Dating Ground Rules, page 148.
- IMPORTANT: Stay positive. If conflicts arise in the conversations, note them, but table them and save for later; don't discuss now!

CHAPTER SUMMARY

How are your lines of communication? Do you say what you mean and mean what you say? Words can help to build an intimate relationship or they can destroy the very foundation of your marriage. It's your choice. By understanding the three patterns of communication, you can choose wisely. Can you share your deepest feelings without attacking your spouse or defending yourself? A simple feelings formula will help you learn to dialogue on a more personal level. A large part of communication is nonverbal (55%) and tone of voice (38%). That only leaves 7 percent for the words! But words are so important! Date Two will help you communicate on a deeper level—you *can* develop the habit of using the companionate pattern of communication. It takes determination, effort, and courage, but you can build a communication system that really works!

DATE TWO EXERCISE

Sharing Our True Feelings

1. What are our favorite topics to talk about? (Things about which we usually agree and promote good interaction)

2. What are our less favorite topics? (Things we tend to debate about)

3. Make a list of "feelings" words that you would feel comfortable using with each other.

4. Take turns answering the following questions:
   How do I feel when:
   - You give me a compliment?

   - You express appreciation for something I did?

   - You smile at me?

   - You make a sacrifice for me?

   - You reach out and touch me?

   - You tell me you love me?

   - You tell me you are proud of me?

POST-DATE APPLICATION

- Keep looking for ways to compliment each other between now and the next date.
- Try to identify when you get into the confrontive pattern of communication and stop before it escalates.
- See how often you can use the companionate pattern.
- Practice using feelings words to better reveal yourself to your spouse.

DATE TWO EXERCISE

Sharing Our True Feelings

1. What are our favorite topics to talk about? (Things about which we usually agree and promote good interaction)

2. What are our less favorite topics? (Things we tend to debate about)

3. Make a list of "feelings" words that you would feel comfortable using with each other.

4. Take turns answering the following questions:
   How do I feel when:
   - You give me a compliment?

   - You express appreciation for something I did?

   - You smile at me?

   - You make a sacrifice for me?

   - You reach out and touch me?

   - You tell me you love me?

   - You tell me you are proud of me?

POST-DATE APPLICATION

- Keep looking for ways to compliment each other between now and the next date.
- Try to identify when you get into the confrontive pattern of communication and stop before it escalates.
- See how often you can use the companionate pattern.
- Practice using feelings words to better reveal yourself to your spouse.

Date Three

Resolving Honest Conflict

PRE-DATE PREPARATION

- Read Chapter 3, "Resolving Honest Conflict." Complete parts 1 and 2 of Date Three Exercise.
- Choose a location that will allow you to talk quietly—perhaps a friend's apartment or a quiet restaurant. Even your local zoo might be fun for this date.

DATE NIGHT TIPS

- Continue to look for new insights about your spouse. This exercise can open new opportunities for growth and intimacy in your marriage.
- Review the communication tips in the Dating Ground Rules with your spouse before you begin discussing the exercise.
- If conflicts arise in the conversations write them down and save for later; but don't try to deal with them on this date!

CHAPTER SUMMARY

Love and anger form a delicate balance in marriage. Love draws us together and anger keeps us from losing our autonomy and becoming enmeshed. But how can we balance the two? Marriage specialist Dr. David Mace says in *Love and Anger in Marriage* that the biggest problem in marriage is not lack of communication, but the inability to handle and process anger. How do you handle anger? Like our animal friends (pages 40–42)? How would you like to handle your anger? Using the feelings formula (from chapter 2) you can express your negative emotions in a way that is not attacking. Once you fully understand how you both feel about an issue, together you can go through the four steps to resolve this issue. Resolution will involve either compromise, capitulation, or coexistence. If you reach a stalemate, the most positive thing you can do is to get help. But in most instances, if you are willing to pull together, to attack the problem and not each other, to process anger and work together at finding a solution, you can find one! Remember when learning how to resolve conflict and process anger, start with an issue that is not too emotional and volatile! After some successes, you can go on to other issues. Remember to top off times of problem solving with times of fun and with reaffirming to each other that you are learning new skills and building an alive marriage!

DATE THREE EXERCISE

PART 1—You and Your Friends at the Zoo

Before your date, rate yourself. Then on your date compare your lists and rankings. Then remember, you don't have to live in the zoo!

1. Which animal character do you identify with the most in handling conflict?
   Rank from the most often used (1) to least often used (5).

   ___ Turtle—The Withdrawer   ___ Chameleon—The Yielder
   ___ Skunk—The Fighter   ___ Owl—The Intellectualizer
   ___ Gorilla—The Winner

To avoid imitating our animal friends, we agree to sign the following anger contract:

Our Anger Contract:

1. We agree to tell each other when we are getting angry.

2. We agree not to vent our anger at each other.

3. We will ask for the other's help in solving whatever is causing the anger.

Signed:_____ Signed:_____

PART 2—Identifying Issues

From Date Two, under "less favorite topics" (the ones you tend to debate), which were the least emotional? List them here:

1. _____

2. _____

3. _____

Compare your list of issues with your mate's list. Together choose one area (preferably the one that is the least emotional) that you think would be easier to resolve than some of the other more emotional ones. Remember to use the feelings formula as you discuss this topic using the companionate pattern of communication.

NOTE: *If you get into a negative pattern and have difficulty at this point, skip to part 4. Later you can choose a time to repeat part 2 and tackle part 3.*

PART 3—Resolving an Issue

From part 2, write out the chosen issue:

The issue we wish to resolve is: _____

Concisely write out how YOU feel about this issue: _____

_____

_____

Exchange exercises and affirm that you really understand how your mate feels. Then you are ready to begin the resolution process. Remember the three C's: Compromise, Capitulation, and Coexistence.

Work through the following four steps:

Step One: Define the problem.

Step Two: Identify who has the need. (which of you feels the great need for a solution and the other person's contribution to the problem).

Step Three: Suggest alternate solutions.

Step Four: Select a plan of action.

PART 4—Having Some Fun!

Enough work for one date! After all, dating is supposed to be fun. Stop on your way home at your favorite ice-cream or yogurt shop and get your favorite dessert! You earned it! Celebrate progress you have made in being able to talk about touchy subjects. And if during the evening, you discovered some really touchy subjects, don't touch them. Instead affirm each other that you are in the process of developing a communication system that really works and you're learning how to process anger in a healthy way.

POST-DATE APPLICATION

- Keep looking for ways to express your feelings without attacking each other or defending yourself.
- See how quickly you can identify when you get into the confrontive pattern of communication, and how fast you can move to the companionate pattern.
- Practice using feelings words to better reveal yourself to your spouse.
- When issues arise, be sure you fully understand each other's feelings before you attempt to find a solution!

DATE THREE EXERCISE

PART 1—You and Your Friends at the Zoo

Before your date, rate yourself. Then on your date compare your lists and rankings. Then remember, you don't have to live in the zoo!

1. Which animal character do you identify with the most in handling conflict?
   Rank from the most often used (1) to least often used (5).

   ___ Turtle—The Withdrawer   ___ Chameleon—The Yielder
   ___ Skunk—The Fighter   ___ Owl—The Intellectualizer
   ___ Gorilla—The Winner

To avoid imitating our animal friends, we agree to sign the following anger contract:

Our Anger Contract:

1. We agree to tell each other when we are getting angry.

2. We agree not to vent our anger at each other.

3. We will ask for the other's help in solving whatever is causing the anger.

Signed:_____ Signed:_____

PART 2—Identifying Issues

From Date Two, under "less favorite topics" (the ones you tend to debate), which were the least emotional? List them here:

1. _____

2. _____

3. _____

Compare your list of issues with your mate's list. Together choose one area (preferably the one that is the least emotional) that you think would be easier to resolve than some of the other more emotional ones. Remember to use the feelings formula as you discuss this topic using the companionate pattern of communication.

NOTE: *If you get into a negative pattern and have difficulty at this point, skip to part 4. Later you can choose a time to repeat part 2 and tackle part 3.*

PART 3—Resolving an Issue

From part 2, write out the chosen issue:

The issue we wish to resolve is: _____

Concisely write out how YOU feel about this issue: _____

_____

_____

Exchange exercises and affirm that you really understand how your mate feels. Then you are ready to begin the resolution process. Remember the three C's: Compromise, Capitulation, and Coexistence.

Work through the following four steps:

Step One: Define the problem.
Step Two: Identify who has the need. (which of you feels the great need for a solution and the other person's contribution to the problem).
Step Three: Suggest alternate solutions.
Step Four: Select a plan of action.

PART 4—Having Some Fun!

Enough work for one date! After all, dating is supposed to be fun. Stop on your way home at your favorite ice-cream or yogurt shop and get your favorite dessert! You earned it! Celebrate progress you have made in being able to talk about touchy subjects. And if during the evening, you discovered some really touchy subjects, don't touch them. Instead affirm each other that you are in the process of developing a communication system that really works and you're learning how to process anger in a healthy way.

POST-DATE APPLICATION

- Keep looking for ways to express your feelings without attacking each other or defending yourself.
- See how quickly you can identify when you get into the confrontive pattern of communication, and how fast you can move to the companionate pattern.
- Practice using feelings words to better reveal yourself to your spouse.
- When issues arise, be sure you fully understand each other's feelings before you attempt to find a solution!

Date Four

Becoming an Encourager

PRE-DATE PREPARATION

- Read Chapter 4, "Becoming an Encourager." Fill out Date Four Exercise.
- Choose a location that will allow you to talk. This might be a good date to combine with something you like to do such as taking a hike, going fishing, playing a set of tennis, going swimming, or bowling.

DATE NIGHT TIPS

- Discuss your exercise, one point at a time.
- Since humor is so important, look for fun and humorous ways to make this date enjoyable. Collect cartoons and surprise your mate!
- This should be one of the easiest dates, so relax and enjoy it!

CHAPTER SUMMARY

Before marriage, it's easy to look for the positive. But once we marry, the stars in our eyes begin to fade and we see each other's idiosyncrasies. The reality of living together creates tension and without realizing what is happening, we can easily focus on the negative instead of the positive. Yet psychologists tell us it takes at least five positive statements to offset one negative statement! We desperately need to develop the habit of looking for the positive and building each other up. Focus on the positive! Date Four will guide you in how to give honest praise by sincerely describing what you appreciate about your spouse. A first cousin of encouragement is humor. Look for ways to laugh together. You will find that laughter relieves tension and is good for the health of your marriage.

DATE FOUR EXERCISE

Becoming an Encourager

To help you develop the habit of encouraging your mate, concentrate on the ways you can sincerely compliment your spouse. Answer the following questions:

1. How has your spouse encouraged you in the past?

2. How would you like your spouse to encourage you in the future?

3. In what areas do you feel most competent?

4. Is there an area that you would like to explore? (Sports, crafts, writing, gourmet cooking, hobbies, education, etc.)

5. What can you do to encourage your spouse to take a risk or try something new?

POST-DATE APPLICATION

- Concentrate, for at least one day, on making sure that your positive statements to your spouse outweigh the negative ones by at least five to one.
- Be gracious and appreciative when your spouse compliments you. And avoid saying, "Oh, you had to do that—it's our assignment!"
- Look for humor!

DATE FOUR EXERCISE

Becoming an Encourager

To help you develop the habit of encouraging your mate, concentrate on the ways you can sincerely compliment your spouse. Answer the following questions:

1. How has your spouse encouraged you in the past?

2. How would you like your spouse to encourage you in the future?

3. In what areas do you feel most competent?

4. Is there an area that you would like to explore? (Sports, crafts, writing, gourmet cooking, hobbies, education, etc.)

5. What can you do to encourage your spouse to take a risk or try something new?

POST-DATE APPLICATION

- Concentrate, for at least one day, on making sure that your positive statements to your spouse outweigh the negative ones by at least five to one.
- Be gracious and appreciative when your spouse compliments you. And avoid saying, "Oh, you had to do that—it's our assignment!"
- Look for humor!

Date Five

Finding Unity in Diversity

PRE-DATE PREPARATION

- Read Chapter 5, "Finding Unity in Diversity." Preview Date Five Exercise.
- Go to your favorite hangout. Again you want to choose a place where you can talk privately.

DATE NIGHT TIPS

- While discussing your exercise, "Balancing Your Seesaws," concentrate on each other's strengths.
- You might want to make a list of your couple strengths. This will help you appreciate how you fill each other's gaps.

CHAPTER SUMMARY

*W*hat are your "couple strengths"? You can discover them by assessing your individual strengths and weaknesses and by encouraging each other to operate in individual areas of strength as much as possible. Batteries of psychological tests are not required. On Date Five you will have the opportunity to talk about the ways you are different and the ways you are alike. Your goal should be to build a strong marriage by benefiting from each other's strengths and appreciating each other's differences. What often happens when we see differences in our spouse is that we react negatively. Often we are so concerned with our spouse's different perspective that we cannot see our own inappropriate reaction. Privately, you may need to go through the four steps of dealing with your own inappropriate reactions (pages 77–78). Then together you can work for unity in your diversity. You can build a strong marriage partnership! You can have an enriched, alive marriage.

DATE FIVE EXERCISE

Balancing Your Strengths and Weaknesses

How are you balancing your marriage in the following areas? In looking at each continuum discuss the following questions:

1. If we are alike, how can we compensate?
2. If we are opposite, how can we balance each other?

Feelings   Facts

Private   Public

Spontaneous   Planner

Active and Assertive   Laid-Back and Calm

Night Owl   Day Lark

Time-Oriented   Not Time-Oriented

POST-DATE APPLICATION

- Look for ways you are different that complement each other.
- In ways that you are alike, look for ways you can compensate!
- If little irritations arise from your differences, privately go through the steps for dealing with your own inappropriate responses (pages 77–78).

DATE FIVE EXERCISE

Balancing Your Strengths and Weaknesses

How are you balancing your marriage in the following areas? In looking at each continuum discuss the following questions:

1. If we are alike, how can we compensate?
2. If we are opposite, how can we balance each other?

Feelings	Facts
Private	Public
Spontaneous	Planner
Active and Assertive	Laid-Back and Calm
Night Owl	Day Lark
Time-Oriented	Not Time-Oriented

POST-DATE APPLICATION

- Look for ways you are different that complement each other.
- In ways that you are alike, look for ways you can compensate!
- If little irritations arise from your differences, privately go through the steps for dealing with your own inappropriate responses (pages 77–78).

Date Six

Building a Creative Love Life

PRE-DATE PREPARATION

- Read Chapter 6, "Building a Creative Love Life." Fill out part 1 of Date Six Exercise.
- If you can plan ahead and go off overnight for this date, bravo! Otherwise, find a quiet place where you can be alone, maybe a friend's empty apartment or condo.

DATE NIGHT TIPS

- While this date is by far the most popular date, it may be the most difficult to talk about. Review chapter 2—especially the part about sharing feelings.
- Think of ways to make this date romantic—holding hands, going for a stroll in the moonlight or for a walk in the rain.

CHAPTER SUMMARY

A fulfilling sexual relationship takes as much work as success in any other area of marriage. Your love life can be influenced by sexual attitudes you brought into your marriage. At each stage of marriage we face challenges in keeping our love life alive. As newlyweds, the challenge is to learn, explore, talk about it, and be other-centered. Throughout marriage a fulfilling sexual relationship takes effort, understanding, and time! Both should feel free to initiate lovemaking. What are you doing to turn your marriage into a love affair? Your sex life can be as fulfilling and exciting as you want to make it. While it takes time and work to be a creative lover, it's worth it. Your love life can become better, more intimate, and more wonderful as the years go by. And a starting place is having Date Six!

DATE SIX EXERCISE

PART 1—Taking the Sexual Attitude Test*

Check the following statements that apply to you. Give yourself one point for each statement checked.

____ I enjoy my sexual relationship with my spouse.

____ I think he/she enjoys it too.

____ I look forward to the next time of physical intimacy.

____ My mate tells me that he/she is satisfied with our sex life.

____ I'm satisfied with our sex life.

____ I initiate lovemaking from time to time.

____ I plan times for us to be alone together.

____ We have had an overnight getaway (alone) in the past six months.

____ I often tell my spouse that I desire him/her.

____ My spouse would describe me as a tender lover.

____ I'm willing to work on areas in our sexual relationship that need improvement.

SCORING: If you checked seven or more of these statements, you most likely have a reasonably good sexual relationship. If your score was lower than seven, don't be discouraged. A candid self-appraisal and an effort to modify your attitude can result in a change in your score in a very short time!

Note: On this test you can miss checking one of the statements and still be a "ten."

---

*The original idea of this SAT came from our friend Kathy Clarke who is a mother, grandmother, and creative lover to her husband, Bill.

PART 2—Planning an Ultimate Getaway*

Plan your own ultimate getaway by answering the following questions:

1. Where would we like to go? Make a list of possible places, then together choose one.

2. When can we go? Write down possible dates for your getaway. Choose one and write it down in your calendar. (You may also want to choose an alternate date.)

3. What are our resources for our getaway? Decide if this will be an economy getaway or the big splurge. Work out a budget and designate funds.

4. What arrangements do we need to make? List things like child care, pet care, reservations, getting directions and maps, preparing food and snacks to take, etc.

5. What should we take with us? Make a packing list of things you want to take along like CD player and your favorite romantic CDs, candles (don't forget matches), snacks, and no work!

6. What are some of the things we would like to do and perhaps talk about during our weekend? Make an appropriate list.

POST-DATE APPLICATION

- Look for ways to make your marriage a love affair.
- Follow up on your initial plans for a getaway. Even twenty-four hours can make a big difference!
- Set guidelines for your getaway:
  1. We will stay positive.
  2. We won't talk about our children or work.
  3. We will leave work and worries at home.
  4. We will have fun!

---

*For a detailed guide for a getaway see our book, *The Ultimate Marriage Builder*, Thomas Nelson, 1994.

DATE SIX EXERCISE

PART 1—Taking the Sexual Attitude Test*

Check the following statements that apply to you. Give yourself one point for each statement checked.

____ I enjoy my sexual relationship with my spouse.

____ I think he/she enjoys it too.

____ I look forward to the next time of physical intimacy.

____ My mate tells me that he/she is satisfied with our sex life.

____ I'm satisfied with our sex life.

____ I initiate lovemaking from time to time.

____ I plan times for us to be alone together.

____ We have had an overnight getaway (alone) in the past six months.

____ I often tell my spouse that I desire him/her.

____ My spouse would describe me as a tender lover.

____ I'm willing to work on areas in our sexual relationship that need improvement.

SCORING: If you checked seven or more of these statements, you most likely have a reasonably good sexual relationship. If your score was lower than seven, don't be discouraged. A candid self-appraisal and an effort to modify your attitude can result in a change in your score in a very short time!

Note: On this test you can miss checking one of the statements and still be a "ten."

---

*The original idea of this SAT came from our friend Kathy Clarke who is a mother, grandmother, and creative lover to her husband, Bill.

PART 2—Planning an Ultimate Getaway*

Plan your own ultimate getaway by answering the following questions:

1. Where would we like to go? Make a list of possible places, then together choose one.

2. When can we go? Write down possible dates for your getaway. Choose one and write it down in your calendar. (You may also want to choose an alternate date.)

3. What are our resources for our getaway? Decide if this will be an economy getaway or the big splurge. Work out a budget and designate funds.

4. What arrangements do we need to make? List things like child care, pet care, reservations, getting directions and maps, preparing food and snacks to take, etc.

5. What should we take with us? Make a packing list of things you want to take along like CD player and your favorite romantic CDs, candles (don't forget matches), snacks, and no work!

6. What are some of the things we would like to do and perhaps talk about during our weekend? Make an appropriate list.

POST-DATE APPLICATION

- Look for ways to make your marriage a love affair.
- Follow up on your initial plans for a getaway. Even twenty-four hours can make a big difference!
- Set guidelines for your getaway:
  1. We will stay positive.
  2. We won't talk about our children or work.
  3. We will leave work and worries at home.
  4. We will have fun!

---

*For a detailed guide for a getaway see our book, *The Ultimate Marriage Builder*, Thomas Nelson, 1994.

Date Seven

Sharing Responsibility and
Working Together

PRE-DATE PREPARATION

- Read Chapter 7, "Sharing Responsibility and Working Together." Look over Date Seven Exercise.
- Choose a location where you can talk. You might want to go out for dinner so neither of you will have to clean the kitchen or wash the dishes.

DATE NIGHT TIPS

- This date doesn't have to be work! Concentrate on finding balance.
- Attack the responsibilities, not each other.
- Use creative brainstorming to find helpful solutions.
- Reward yourself by ordering dessert.

CHAPTER SUMMARY

*I*sn't it time someone took out the garbage?" is more than a trite question. Divvying up household chores is a real issue for married couples—especially for those who are trying to balance jobs outside the home. You can begin by assessing your present responsibilities and making any adjustments that are needed to bring more balance into your lives. Also helpful is defining and evaluating your financial goals. By choosing your own lifestyle carefully, you may discover that, when considering quality of life, less is more. Take advantage of Date Seven to look at your present situation and responsibilities; evaluate each person's contribution to both problems with and solutions for balancing your two-job tightrope. You may discover that working with your mate can be one of your most rewarding jobs! Especially if you pull together!

DATE SEVEN EXERCISE

PART 1—Assessing and Balancing Your Responsibilities

1. Assess your present responsibilities:

    List your responsibilities outside the home:
    Husband   Wife

    _____   _____
    _____   _____
    _____   _____
    _____   _____
    _____   _____

    List your responsibilities inside the home:
    Husband   Wife

    _____   _____
    _____   _____
    _____   _____
    _____   _____

2. Consider how you can balance home responsibilities:

    List all household jobs and responsibilities such as preparing meals, cleaning the house, doing the laundry, helping the children with homework, caring for the yard:
    Husband   Wife

    _____   _____
    _____   _____
    _____   _____
    _____   _____
    _____   _____

    From the list above choose the jobs you prefer to do:
    Husband   Wife

    _____   _____
    _____   _____
    _____   _____
    _____   _____

Brainstorm solutions for the jobs that are on neither of your lists: (remember the three C's: Compromise, Capitulation, and Coexistence.) Include your children in your planning as well. Choose age-appropriate chores to help lighten your burden. For more help choosing chores for your children, we recommend the book *Children Who Do Too Little* by Patricia Sprinkle (Zondervan).

Our plan is: _____

_____

_____

_____

PART 2—Managing Time Pressures

Answer the following questions to help evaluate how you are dealing with time pressures in your marriage relationship:

1. Do I feel in control of my time?
2. Do I try to avoid overscheduling?
3. Do I set limits on my work?
4. Am I getting enough sleep and eating a balanced diet?
5. Am I punctual when meeting my spouse?
6. Do I watch more than one hour of television each day?
7. Do I have time for friends and family?
8. Do I have any leisure time?
9. Do I spend enough time with my children?
10. Do I have any private time for reflection and meditation?

Talk through your lists and discuss what changes you need to make and which ones are realistic.

POST-DATE APPLICATION

- Monitor your new plans for working together.
- Compliment your spouse when he or she accomplishes a new task.
- You might want to choose a question each day from part 2, the exercise on managing time pressures, and talk about how you are doing.
- Have the mind-set that you are going to work together. It can make a big difference in your attitude and outlook on life!

DATE SEVEN EXERCISE

PART 1—Assessing and Balancing Your Responsibilities

1. Assess your present responsibilities:

    List your responsibilities outside the home:

Husband	Wife
_____	_____
_____	_____
_____	_____
_____	_____
_____	_____

    List your responsibilities inside the home:

Husband	Wife
_____	_____
_____	_____
_____	_____
_____	_____
_____	_____

2. Consider how you can balance home responsibilities:

    List all household jobs and responsibilities such as preparing meals, cleaning the house, doing the laundry, helping the children with homework, caring for the yard:

Husband	Wife
_____	_____
_____	_____
_____	_____
_____	_____
_____	_____

    From the list above choose the jobs you prefer to do:

Husband	Wife
_____	_____
_____	_____
_____	_____
_____	_____

Brainstorm solutions for the jobs that are on neither of your lists: (remember the three C's: Compromise, Capitulation, and Coexistence.) Include your children in your planning as well. Choose age-appropriate chores to help lighten your burden. For more help choosing chores for your children, we recommend the book *Children Who Do Too Little* by Patricia Sprinkle (Zondervan).

Our plan is: _____

_____

_____

_____

PART 2—Managing Time Pressures

Answer the following questions to help evaluate how you are dealing with time pressures in your marriage relationship:

1. Do I feel in control of my time?
2. Do I try to avoid overscheduling?
3. Do I set limits on my work?
4. Am I getting enough sleep and eating a balanced diet?
5. Am I punctual when meeting my spouse?
6. Do I watch more than one hour of television each day?
7. Do I have time for friends and family?
8. Do I have any leisure time?
9. Do I spend enough time with my children?
10. Do I have any private time for reflection and meditation?

Talk through your lists and discuss what changes you need to make and which ones are realistic.

POST-DATE APPLICATION

- Monitor your new plans for working together.
- Compliment your spouse when he or she accomplishes a new task.
- You might want to choose a question each day from part 2, the exercise on managing time pressures, and talk about how you are doing.
- Have the mind-set that you are going to work together. It can make a big difference in your attitude and outlook on life!

Date Eight

Balancing Your Roles
As Partner and Parent

PRE-DATE PREPARATION

- Read Chapter 8, "Balancing Your Roles as Partner and Parent." Be prepared to discuss Date Eight Exercise.
- Choose a location where you can be far away from your children! You might want to do something physical like taking a long walk.

DATE NIGHT TIPS

- Remember your children will grow up and leave home, but your spouse is there for life!
- Keep the focus on your marriage and how children affect your relationship.
- This is not a time to try to solve your children's problems or to talk about discipline, school work, or curfews!
- Talk about the parents—that's you!

CHAPTER SUMMARY

*E*nriching your marriage while parenting your children is not an oxymoron even though it seems like one. Your role as a partner does not have to compete with your role as a parent. However, balancing both roles requires much skill and may leave you tired just thinking about it! It helps to realize the ways children can enrich your marriage. For instance, they are a continual reminder that you're one; they foster teamwork and creativity as you scrape to find time together; and they check your own communication. At the same time, when you take seriously the challenge to build an alive, enriched marriage, you will enrich your children's lives and future marriages. You are their model for how

to build healthy relationships. You teach them life skills and pass on traditions and values. On Date Eight as you talk about how can you balance your dual roles as partner and parent, remember you are passing
on a heritage of healthy relationships to future generations.

DATE EIGHT EXERCISE

PART 1—How Our Children Enrich Our Marriage

Discuss the following statements and list ways each is true in your marriage.

1. Children remind us that we're one.
2. Children foster teamwork.
3. Children promote appreciation.
4. Children promote creativity.
5. Children check our communication and keep us honest.
6. Children prevent boredom.
7. Children give great rewards.

PART 2—How Our Marriage Enriches Our Children

Discuss the following statements and list ways each is true in your marriage.

1. We provide security, love, and a sense of belonging.
2. We model healthy relationships.
3. We give guidance and leadership.
4. We teach life skills.
5. We pass on traditions and values.

PART 3—Family Planning

(for couples considering having a family)

Discuss the following questions:

1. How many children would I like to have?
2. What would be the ideal spacing of children?
3. What are my favorite names? How do I feel about family names?
4. How do I feel about child care?
5. How can we still find time for two?
6. What is my concept of "coparenting"?

POST-DATE APPLICATION

- Look for the positive ways your children impact your marriage.
- Look for the positive ways your marriage impacts your children.

DATE EIGHT EXERCISE

PART 1—How Our Children Enrich Our Marriage

Discuss the following statements and list ways each is true in your marriage.

1. Children remind us that we're one.
2. Children foster teamwork.
3. Children promote appreciation.
4. Children promote creativity.
5. Children check our communication and keep us honest.
6. Children prevent boredom.
7. Children give great rewards.

PART 2—How Our Marriage Enriches Our Children

Discuss the following statements and list ways each is true in your marriage.

1. We provide security, love, and a sense of belonging.
2. We model healthy relationships.
3. We give guidance and leadership.
4. We teach life skills.
5. We pass on traditions and values.

PART 3—Family Planning
(for couples considering having a family)

Discuss the following questions:

1. How many children would I like to have?
2. What would be the ideal spacing of children?
3. What are my favorite names? How do I feel about family names?
4. How do I feel about child care?
5. How can we still find time for two?
6. What is my concept of "coparenting"?

POST-DATE APPLICATION

- Look for the positive ways your children impact your marriage.
- Look for the positive ways your marriage impacts your children.

Date Nine

Developing Spiritual Intimacy

PRE-DATE PREPARATION

- Read Chapter 9, "Developing Spiritual Intimacy." Preview Date Nine Exercise.
- Choose a location where you can quietly reflect together. You might even want to go to a church that is open to the public.

DATE NIGHT TIPS

- If you are at different places on your spiritual journey, be sensitive to one another.
- Talk about what you have in common.
- This is an opportunity to share your inner feelings. It is not a time to try to change your spouse.

CHAPTER SUMMARY

Sharing core beliefs and living out these beliefs in your marriage can foster a wonderful type of intimacy—spiritual intimacy. It is important to first understand your own belief system, which includes your values, ethics, and any religious beliefs, and then find the common bonds between you as a couple. These commonalities will form the foundation for your shared belief system and are the springboard for developing a spiritual dimension to your relationship. Spiritual intimacy manifests itself in unconditional love and acceptance, forgiveness, prayer, and service to others.

DATE NINE EXERCISE

Developing Spiritual Intimacy

Discuss the following questions:

1. Individually and as a couple, where are you on your spiritual pilgrimage?

2. What are your basic core beliefs?

3. In what ways do you live out spiritual intimacy?

4. What could you do to serve others?

POST-DATE APPLICATION

- Together write a list of your shared core beliefs.
- Pick one book on a topic related to spiritual growth and commit to read it together in the coming year.

DATE NINE EXERCISE

Developing Spiritual Intimacy

Discuss the following questions:

1. Individually and as a couple, where are you on your spiritual pilgrimage?

2. What are your basic core beliefs?

3. In what ways do you live out spiritual intimacy?

4. What could you do to serve others?

POST-DATE APPLICATION

- Together write a list of your shared core beliefs.
- Pick one book on a topic related to spiritual growth and commit to read it together in the coming year.

Date Ten

Having an Intentional Marriage

PRE-DATE PREPARATION

- Read Chapter 10, "Having an Intentional Marriage." Fill out Date Ten Exercise.
- Choose a location where you can have access to a table. Your local library might be a fun place for this date. You would have access to many resources as you plan your intentional marriage!

DATE NIGHT TIPS

- Take your time; don't race through this date.
- Set at least one goal that you both want to achieve, but don't be overambitious. It's better to reach one goal than to have ten that you don't reach.

CHAPTER SUMMARY

You can have an intentional marriage by reviewing your past expectations, evaluating your present marriage involvement style, and setting goals for your future, being careful to monitor your progress toward your goals. A common problem in marriage is conflicting needs, but if you don't understand each other's needs, you can't address them. It may help to think about what expectations you brought into marriage and decide which ones were realistic and which ones have been met. What is your marriage involvement style? (See pages 125–128.) If you and your spouse were each represented by individual circles, how much would your circles overlap? How much do you desire your lives to overlap? Do you desire minimum, moderate, or maximum involvement? All three marriage involvement styles can work, if you both agree on the amount of involvement you desire. Once you understand your expectations and desired involvement, you can set realistic goals for your marriage. Then, to put feet on your goals, answer the three questions: what, how, and when? Date Ten will help you turn your desires and dreams for your marriage into reality!

DATE TEN EXERCISE

PART 1—Expectation Survey*

What are your expectations? Why did you get married? What is most important to you and your mate? Let's look at seven areas of expectations in marriage. Rank them in order of their importance to you (1 for very important; 7 for unimportant). Then go back through the list and rank them according to their importance to your spouse.

___ ___ 1. **Security**—The knowledge of permanence in the relationship and of financial and material well-being.

___ ___ 2. **Companionship**—Having a friend who goes through all the joys and sorrows of life with you, a soul partner; having common areas of interest.

___ ___ 3. **Sex**—The oneness that comes through physical intimacy in marriage; the initiation and enjoyment of a growing love relationship.

___ ___ 4. **Understanding and tenderness**—Experiencing regularly the touch, the kiss, the winks across the room that say, "I love you," "I care," "I'm thinking of you."

___ ___ 5. **Encouragement**—Having someone verbally support and appreciate your work and efforts in your profession, in your home, with the children, and so on.

___ ___ 6. **Intellectual closeness**—Discussing and growing together in common areas of intellectual thought.

___ ___ 7. **Mutual activity**—Doing things together—politics, sports, church work, hobbies.

PART 2—Degrees of Involvement in Marriage

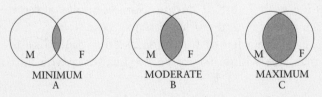

1. Where would you place your marriage—A, B, or C?

---

*Expectation Survey was adapted from: Mary Susan Miller, "What are Your Expectations from Marriage?" *Family Life Today* (October 1980), 19.

2. Which degree of involvement would you like to have in your marriage?
3. What is realistic for you at this stage of your marriage?

PART 3—Setting Realistic Goals

To set realistic goals for your marriage, consider the following three questions:

1. In Part 1 of this exercise, how far apart are your expectations? Have you identified some expectations that you'd like to meet?
2. In Part 2 of this exercise, how involved do you want to be with each other? What style of marriage do you want?
3. How can you devise a plan of action to get where you want to be? List possible goals:

_____

_____

_____

_____

Answer three questions:
1. WHAT? (choose one goal)
2. HOW? (things you will do to help accomplish your goal)
3. WHEN? (write in your calendar!)

POST-DATE APPLICATION

- Follow your new intentional marriage plan.
- Keep an intentional marriage journal and monitor your progress. For instance, "Today we got up ten minutes early for our couple-sharing time. It was so meaningful, we plan to repeat it tomorrow!"
- Keep looking for the positive and complimenting each other. (By now, this should be a habit.)
- Continue your habit of dating. Some couples agree to go back through these ten dates at least once a year.
- Together make a list of future dates you would like to have. An alive marriage will remain alive and healthy as you nurture it.

DATE TEN EXERCISE

PART 1—Expectation Survey*

What are your expectations? Why did you get married? What is most important to you and your mate? Let's look at seven areas of expectations in marriage. Rank them in order of their importance to you (1 for very important; 7 for unimportant). Then go back through the list and rank them according to their importance to your spouse.

___ ___ 1. **Security**—The knowledge of permanence in the relationship and of financial and material well-being.

___ ___ 2. **Companionship**—Having a friend who goes through all the joys and sorrows of life with you, a soul partner; having common areas of interest.

___ ___ 3. **Sex**—The oneness that comes through physical intimacy in marriage; the initiation and enjoyment of a growing love relationship.

___ ___ 4. **Understanding and tenderness**—Experiencing regularly the touch, the kiss, the winks across the room that say, "I love you," "I care," "I'm thinking of you."

___ ___ 5. **Encouragement**—Having someone verbally support and appreciate your work and efforts in your profession, in your home, with the children, and so on.

___ ___ 6. **Intellectual closeness**—Discussing and growing together in common areas of intellectual thought.

___ ___ 7. **Mutual activity**—Doing things together—politics, sports, church work, hobbies.

PART 2—Degrees of Involvement in Marriage

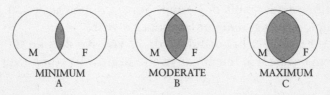

1. Where would you place your marriage—A, B, or C?

---

*Expectation Survey was adapted from: Mary Susan Miller, "What are Your Expectations from Marriage?" *Family Life Today* (October 1980), 19.

2. Which degree of involvement would you like to have in your marriage?
3. What is realistic for you at this stage of your marriage?

PART 3—Setting Realistic Goals

To set realistic goals for your marriage, consider the following three questions:

1. In Part 1 of this exercise, how far apart are your expectations? Have you identified some expectations that you'd like to meet?
2. In Part 2 of this exercise, how involved do you want to be with each other? What style of marriage do you want?
3. How can you devise a plan of action to get where you want to be? List possible goals:

_____

_____

_____

Answer three questions:
1. WHAT? (choose one goal)
2. HOW? (things you will do to help accomplish your goal)
3. WHEN? (write in your calendar!)

POST-DATE APPLICATION

- Follow your new intentional marriage plan.
- Keep an intentional marriage journal and monitor your progress. For instance, "Today we got up ten minutes early for our couple-sharing time. It was so meaningful, we plan to repeat it tomorrow!"
- Keep looking for the positive and complimenting each other. (By now, this should be a habit.)
- Continue your habit of dating. Some couples agree to go back through these ten dates at least once a year.
- Together make a list of future dates you would like to have. An alive marriage will remain alive and healthy as you nurture it.